JACOB'S
BLESSING

DONNA SINCLAIR &
CHRISTOPHER WHITE

JACOB'S BLESSING

DREAMS, HOPES, & VISIONS FOR THE CHURCH

WOOD LAKE BOOKS

Editors: James Taylor and Michael Schwartzentruber
Cover art and design: Margaret Kyle
Interior design: Julie Bachewich and Margaret Kyle
Consulting art director: Robert MacDonald

We acknowledge the financial support of the Government of Canada through the
Book Publishing Industry Development Program (BPIDP) for our publishing
activities.   Canadä

At WOOD LAKE BOOKS we practice what we publish, guided by a concern for fairness, justice, and
equal opportunity in all of our relationships with employees and customers.

Wood Lake Books Inc. is committed to caring for the environment and all creation. We recycle,
reuse and compost, and encourage readers to do the same. Resources are printed on recycled
paper and more environmentally friendly groundwood papers (newsprint), whenever possible. A
portion of all profit is donated to charitable organizations.

Canadian Cataloguing in Publication Data
Sinclair, Donna, 1943-
Jacob's blessing
Includes bibliographical references.
ISBN 1-55145-381-9
1. Protestant churches – Canada. 2. Church renewal – Canada. 3. Postmodernism – Religious
aspects – Protestant churches. I. White, Christopher. II. Title.
BR115.W6S56 1999   280'.4'0971   C99-910961-8

Published by Wood Lake Books
Kelowna, British Columbia, Canada

Printing 9 8 7 6 5 4 3 2 1
Printed in Canada by Transcontinental Printing

Contents

To Jim Sinclair
whose love of church is matched
by his delight in life.

To Wendy Hedderwick-White,
for making my dreams come true.

Acknowledgments

The people, and especially the choir, of St. Andrew's United in North Bay, Ontario, have supported me tenderly through other books, but never more than through this one. I am grateful for the way they are church to me.

When Christopher White phoned to ask me to co-author this book, I mumbled "Mm, well, maybe," the first and even the second time. I'm glad he persisted. We worked hard; and we discovered that pouring love for the church and ideas for its renewal into a suitable container (like this one) is a tremendously exciting, fulfilling task.

My friends have once again cheerfully survived conversations that constantly begin and end with "I was just writing that..." and "As soon as this book is done..." To Wanda, Kathy, Rose, Sarah, Muriel, Trish (to name the ones who heard these phrases most often) I am, as always, grateful.

My children, David, Andy, and Tracy, have always remembered to ask "How's the book?" And then they actually listened to my reply. I am grateful for this confirmation of my belief that Jim and I raised them properly.

I am grateful for my mother's calm certitude that there will be insights in this book.

I am grateful to Terry Dokis for the labyrinth, and his ability to reach across cultures in kindness.

Jim Taylor was one of my first editors, 30 years ago. He is the editor of this book. I was grateful for his knowledge and sensitivity then, and I am grateful now.

Many stories in this book came to me first as a Senior Writer at *The United Church Observer*. I am, as always, grateful to my colleagues for their wisdom and perspective; and for the way they sustain a wonderful magazine that helps United Church people understand the world through the eyes of faith.

The staff of Wood Lake Books have been unusually engaged with this book as it evolved – especially in the creation of the study guide and video *Weaving a Congregational Tapestry,* in which some of the themes of this book are discussed, and in their skilled leadership at workshops across Canada with that same title. Cheryl Perry and Mike Schwartzentruber began the editing process. I am grateful for the enthusiasm and care of all these people.

Jim Sinclair has always shown me how exciting the church is, even in the midst of massive change. I am grateful for his strength, and sense of humor, and love.

– DONNA SINCLAIR

Over two years ago I decided that I wanted to write a book on the future of the church. I was dissatisfied with some of what I was reading and wanted to add my ideas to the mix.

But I wanted, and needed, to launch this project as part of a team, to give the book the depth I felt it deserved. I had read Donna Sinclair's work for a number of years and thought that she was just the person I needed. So I gave her a call (a number of calls, actually) and she agreed to participate. It was one of my better decisions.

Donna has been a joy to work with. I have learned a great deal writing with her, and she has been generous with her wisdom and her talent. I am a better writer, and the book has a balance and perspective that has made it infinitely richer, because of her.

I want also to thank Mike Schwartzentruber who began editing this work, and Jim Taylor who completed the bulk of the task. Both of them strengthened this book with their critiques, ideas, and support. At times we strove like Jacob and the angel, but emerged the better for it.

My thanks go to my colleagues: Sandra Bath, our church secretary; and Gail Brimbecom, our parish nurse. Sandra has kept me on track as I've juggled a busy parish while writing and Gail's ministry here at Westminster has been a critical support to me this past year.

Joan Sanderson from Westminster has been an invaluable resource in writing this book. I thank her for her ideas and input, and for constantly challenging me to think in new directions.

Countless people spoke to me during the writing of this book and were generous with their time and ideas.

Thanks also to my good friend Bob Thaler. His calls, letters, and monthly lunches have helped keep me sane!

Jacob's Blessing has arisen from my work with two congregations: Springbank United in Calgary, Alberta, where I served as a new ordinand from 1987–1992, and Westminster United in Whitby, Ontario, where I currently minister. To the people of Springbank, thank you for taking me and my family into your hearts. You let me try my wings, were patient, supportive, and introduced me to the wonders of sheep on Christmas Eve! To Westminster, I hardly know how to say thank you. Over the years we have grown together and experienced tremendous change. We have worked together with faith, humor, and joy. I have great fun being your minister and we continue to learn from each other. My family and I have been greatly blessed through our shared ministry. This book is your story, as much as mine.

Finally, thanks to my family. My wife, Wendy, has always supported me and been the rudder of our ship on our 20-year adventure together, be it in Africa, Alberta, or Ontario. My father, Prof. Patrick C. T. White, taught me how to write and encouraged me to do so. My mom, Jane Denis White, once had a dream and lives on in our hearts. And my girls, Sarah and Elizabeth, are my inspiration and my joy.

— CHRISTOPHER WHITE

Introduction

It's been a tough two decades for the mainline church. Numbers decline; congregations merge and close; a sorry parade of statistics forecasts the end of the church as we know it.

Society proclaims an intense interest in "spirituality." Yet at the same time the local church experiences an exodus from the pews and disinterest from the general population. Society as a whole seems to ignore us. The mass media give us coverage only when scandals, fiscal and sexual, raise their ugly heads.

It's too bad. At its best, the Christian church feeds the hungry and stands up for the poor. It was present in internment camps when Japanese-Canadians were removed from their homes in World War II; today, it fights for refugees and the ozone layer with equal passion. Most of all, it allows people, in a unique way, to converse with a mysterious and loving God.

Despite all this, a local CBC radio morning host recently remarked that that he doesn't "know anybody who goes to church anymore." The news is so gloomy that it would take the heart out of the most optimistic of us.

Only me and thee

Our varied denominations have responded to the decline of the past decades by dividing into two distinct and opposite camps.

The first camp embraces what has became known as the "faithful remnant" theory. This theory argues that our decline is a natural result of living in a post-modern, post-Christian society. Since Christianity has ceased to be the *de facto* state religion, people are no longer socially obliged to attend church. Thus, the wheat has been separated from the chaff and only the faithful remnant – that is, those who truly believe – remain.

For this group, growth equates with heresy. If your congregation is growing, you may have sold out to the consumer society; you are probably not "faithful" to issues of social justice or the gospel.

There are variations on the "faithful remnant" theory. Some writers, such as Marva Dawn, support a return to tradition as a way out of our current malaise. Others, such as John Shelby Spong, advocate a complete redefinition of the Christian faith if the Church is to survive the next 25 years.

The faithful remnant thesis has been falling out of favor recently. Denominational church leaders used to find it comforting – it excused them from fault as membership and givings declined. But they have had to bear the brunt of reduced revenues through job loss and constant program cutbacks. Critical issues around social justice need adequate funding; when that funding erodes, the ability of the church to help those in need gets caught in a spiral of cuts. The institutional church cannot survive as a faithful remnant.

And the news isn't going to get any better.

The people who have sustained the general funds of our churches over the decades have had strong denominational ties. But their numbers decrease with every year. Younger members of congregations do not feel the same institutional loyalty. They will direct the bulk of their stewardship toward the local congregation or other causes, not the national church.

There is a gap (some would call it a chasm) between pew and head office. As budgets for travel decrease and homogeneity of belief disappears, the fate of denominational headquarters comes into question. In many denominations, the church's own structure and governance suggests the trend will continue. A major redefinition of denomination is required.

In fact, people are no longer attached to denominational labels. They simply seek a place that feels like home. While this is more true in the United States than in Canada, the trend is comparable. In the suburban community of Whitby, just east of Toronto, Ontario, where Christopher White ministers, the congregation has a rich mix of all ages, but with an emphasis on young families. A typical Sunday gathering for worship includes Baptists, Catholics, Lutherans, Presbyterians, and Anglicans, in addition to those with their roots firmly in the United Church of Canada. Stewardship for the national church's Mission and Service Fund is a difficult sell in that religious mosaic.

Donna Sinclair attends St. Andrew's United in North Bay, in northern Ontario. Many people attend because that's where they were baptized and married, and where their children were confirmed. But others are there — from widely assorted backgrounds — because they feel drawn to the church's strong social justice stance, to its determination to "be with" those whose voices are seldom heard, and to its pastoral care and liturgy.

All over the continent, there are congregations like these, where the traditional attender anchored in the history of the place mixes with — and sometimes embraces — the newer members. It requires ongoing but rewarding work in both integration and education.

Opening up the Big Box

The second response to the decline of the mainline denominations is changing the face of church life across North America. As retailers have moved to the "big box" model with warehouse stores to draw in customers, so too have some churches. Recent decades have witnessed the explosion of the megachurch — huge multi-staffed transdenominational congregations that dwarf the traditional neighborhood church.

Built on a model of small groups meeting during the week for fellowship and education, coupled with mass assemblies for contemporary worship, these congregations reach thousands of people every Sunday. Conservative theology, upbeat music, staff trained for many needs, and the intimacy of small groups seems to be a winning formula. The Willow Creek Association, one of the first of these megachurches, and the Vineyard Fellowships have evolved into a new kind of denomination, creating new loyalties and affiliations.

Ministers and committed laypeople, tired and frustrated with the decline of their local neighborhood church, optimistically visit new-formula churches: Willow Creek outside Chicago or Saddleback Community

Church in southern California. They return from a church that brings in 15,000 people on a Sunday to a church that draws, on the average, less than one percent of that number. A study by World Vision Canada found that two-thirds of Canadian churches have 125 or fewer worshippers on a Sunday morning; more than half of these have 75 or fewer. Few Canadian churches can seat – let alone attract – 1000 people on a Sunday. (In the U.S., those statistics can be roughly doubled.) They then try to introduce a model that does not fit their local church's culture or history, and are inevitably disappointed and frustrated when it founders.

It fails for a variety of reasons. A major one is that the megachurch concentrates on a particular age range – the baby boomers and Generation X. Worship becomes exclusive. Multiple generations do not worship together.

How can we be one if we are divided by generational tastes?

Church and society alike need the wisdom of age, the enthusiasm of youth, and the restless searching of the middle years. A vital church cannot be either an adults-only retirement complex or a yuppie recreation center. It needs to be more like a village – with all the joys and frustrations that come with small-town life.

All too often, neighborhood and rural churches become private clubs where newcomers are welcome only if they understand the rules, the language, and the way that things are done. Congregations exclude people by refusing to change, by not being open to new ideas, and by wishing fruitlessly that things could be the way that they were in the good old days when churches were full and society seemed (but wasn't) less complex.

So what's the future for the neighborhood church or the rural multipoint parish? Is decline inevitable? Twenty years from now, will only mega churches, with a smattering of mainline congregations, be left on the landscape?

A hopeful alternative

We believe that there is another possibility that is not limited to the two options outlined here. It is a way that is faithful, but that still allows congregations to thrive and possibly even grow. It permits us to speak of justice and live with mystery. It seeks to understand what has gone before, and integrates our history into what is coming.

It is a way that arises out of who we are.

We have entered a time of globalization and incredibly rapid transformation, a time where the volume of technological change doubles every 20 months, where trillions of dollars are traded every day, and economies and whole societies are left reeling in the wake of global financial instability. Yet it is also a time of opportunity for the church.

Both the New Testament and subsequent church history teach us the innate strength of the local congregation. It has survived the rise and fall of empires and nation states. It has survived wars, plagues, and famines. It was born in an agricultural era, and made the transition into an industrial age. There is no reason to believe it will succumb to a post-industrial information age.

Every Sunday, people gather together to worship God and proclaim the resurrection of Jesus. Canadian sociologist Reginald Bibby notes that, despite sagging attendance figures, more still attend church each Sunday than the total number of fans who attend the home games of the Toronto Blue Jays baseball team in an entire season![1]

A story (significantly, passed along on an Internet site) told of a Hindu social worker's conversation with Ruth Isabel Seabury, one of the great missionary educators of this past century. The Hindu said of the Christian congregation:

A congregation is never just an audience. It's never just people sitting in a row, listening, praying, worshipping. It's a little group made one in the power of its Savior. It has to learn to make its way into the world as a moving power.

I have seen all across your country Mr. So-and-so's pulpit, and heard talk of the great size of his audience! I have seen you count the effectiveness of the Church by numbers. I have heard Christians weigh the church's worth by the total of its resources and the richness of its property, and I have said to myself, "But what has this to do with the congregation, that little welded fellowship in which the power works?"

For you see, the power of the Savior must be in the congregation, driving them out to meet the rest of humankind. That's the way he reaches the world.[2]

Something new being born

We, the authors of this book, see something new being born in congregations all over North America. What has gone before may be dying, but it must die for the new church to be born. We are not clear what the new church will look like, but we expect it will be different for each community. In a world of constant change and growing diversity, there is no single template for thriving congregations. No one model fits all.

So this is not a how-to book, not a recipe for adding this program and that ministry and, bingo! instant church. Instead we attempt to reflect on the crucial passage that is taking place. As journalist and minister, both of us passionately committed to the church, we explore the new self-understandings that – sometimes painfully – have come to us in the last two decades.

In 1999, we tried out a few of these ideas on some people who attended a workshop called Weaving Congregational Tapestry, at Crieff Hills, a Presbyterian retreat center in Ontario. We paid very careful attention to the response of that group. It was abundantly clear that many people, in many congregations, large and small, are deeply committed to defining a solid vision of church for our time.

The tough decades are far from over. But we confidently declare that the church will be reborn, and that the new birth will start with local congregations. Sometimes the church that is arriving will look a lot like the old one, and other times will be unrecognizable. If it survives the trauma of its birth (and we believe it will), it will be more whole. It will know its weaknesses and will not be frightened by them. Above all, in a society that often seems devoted to the pursuit of individual gain, it will recognize its own value as the carrier of memory and compassion, mystery and love, song and prayer.

A Worthy Lineage

DONNA SINCLAIR

Jacob was left alone;
and a man wrestled with him until daybreak.
Genesis 32:24

The story of Jacob who wrestles with the stranger consumes exactly half of the Book of Genesis. It is full of intrigue and heartbreak, disappointment and fear, reconciliation and joy. That's why it has endured. Jacob's passion and hope are the elements of human life.

But in an eerily specific way, it is also the story of the North American Christian church at this moment. In what we happily used to call the "mainline" denominations, we struggle with the unknown in the darkness. While some congregations flourish, attendance is down in the majority and gray heads predominate. Finances are slipping. Where the large denominations once had the ear of cabinet ministers, the secular world now ignores these denominations, or – with the exception of a few television shows – portrays them as quaint. Our members are not of one mind: gay ordination, women's rights, peace issues, the nature of Jesus, the very language we use to address God, the hymns we will or will not sing – these matters divide us, sometimes even within the same congregation.

Like Jacob, we don't know how to name what is happening to us, we don't know if we will see daybreak, and we fear what tomorrow will bring.

But we are granted occasional glimpses of the future.

Knowing instinctively

Not long ago I arrived – very late – for a planning meeting for a women's congregational retreat that I had agreed to lead. The little group had already decided how it would be. They would begin with singing, they said, "at least three-quarters of an hour of it. Our lives are busy and we need it."

Then I was to talk – not about the future of the church or any of the small bits of information that I acquire in my profession as a journalist – but about prayer. And we would actually do that, pray, for quite a while.

Fine, I agreed.

In the afternoon we would braid sweetgrass. It was already being collected from various fields nearby. We would have a sweetgrass ceremony, would I want to lead…?

"No," I assured them hastily, "I am white, and I am afraid it would be disrespectful."

They discussed whether one of them could lead – one planner is Native, and reclaiming her heritage – but agreed they would invite a guest who had been learning for a long time from an elder.

They requested an Easter story.

"You mean, about the tomb and the angels," I said.

"No, no," they replied, "not *that* Easter story. This is June, not April. We mean a story about someone, a woman, who has undergone a great crisis and rises again."

"And we'll close with a Taizé service," they said.

"I don't actually know how to do that," I responded weakly.

No matter. Although I had not attended any of the Taizé services our congregation has held many Sunday evenings in the last two years, they had. All was in hand.

In this encounter, I believe I received a glimpse of the new church that is being born. The women at that meeting were perfectly aware of their spiritual needs. They knew that we all need lots of singing, lots of letting the words and music of praise and joy soothe us. They knew that the great Christian story of dying and rising, death and rebirth, still plays out in the lives of women today. They knew it is not locked in the past. They knew how to draw on each other's strengths. They knew they wanted to integrate the traditions of this land, long ignored, into their worship. They also knew how to take what they wanted (the Taizé liturgies, for instance) from other traditions. They understood that our whole beings, body and soul, all five senses and more, come to church. So they would have candles and flowers and fabric and music and food, and the wonderful smell of sweet grass.

And we were all lay people, a fact which went entirely unremarked, as if it was of no consequence – although if any ordained or commissioned persons had appeared, their strengths would have been gently called forth.

I don't believe the church of tomorrow will necessarily look just like that. But it will have the kind of freedom and wholeness these women exemplified.

Jacob's blessing

This book contains some small glances at tomorrow – like that one – that are rising in congregations today. It also contains backward looks at the past. Like Jacob heading out for home, we need to know where we have come from, to recognize where we are going – because the North American Christian church *is* in the process of being transformed. As Christians, we are being given a new identity, one so unfamiliar we may have trouble recognizing ourselves.

But we can learn about new identity, about transformation, from Jacob.

This is how Jacob's story goes. (You can look up a less idiosyncratic version in Genesis, chapters 25 to 50, if you wish.)

The infant Jacob is born clutching his twin brother's heel – a grasper right from the beginning. He grows up to be the quiet one, the son who prefers the serenity of the tent to the hunt, the bee-humming garden over hard days in the wilderness chasing the deer his father Isaac prefers to legumes and fruit.

But he is what we might call "street smart." In his silence, there is a canny ability to focus on the future. When his twin, Esau the hunter, arrives home half-starved, Jacob barters a simple lentil soup for the rights Esau enjoys as the eldest son. Either Jacob is the world's finest cook or – more likely – Esau lives so deeply in the present moment that only his gnawing stomach matters to him.

Later, when Jacob tricks blind old Isaac out of the blessing that – again – should have been the elder son's by right of birth, Jacob realizes it would be prudent to flee before his father dies and he is left to his sibling's not-too-tender mercies.

It's not hard to see why this story would endure. Jacob is a classic introvert, a totally different personality type from Esau. Any congregation will have some of both – the get-things-done-now types, and the wait-and-see, thoughtful, planning types.

And Jacob's mindset is so modern, too. Who says the inheritance should always go to the eldest? Who says a father should have only one blessing? Don't we, these days, admire those persons who seek to change the rules and better their lot in life?

Jacob flees to his mother's family where he immediately falls in love with his cousin Rachel, who, scripture tells us, is "graceful and beautiful." In what must be one of history's earliest put-downs, her older sister is described thus: "Leah's eyes were lovely."

Here we discover that Jacob's trickster habits run in the family. His uncle Laban gets him to work seven years for Rachel's hand in marriage only to substitute Leah on the wedding night. Laban then smooths over this deception by suggesting, "In our country, we don't marry off the younger before the first-born."

Once again, the presumed rights of the elder child trip Jacob up. So he works another seven years to pay for Rachel.

I remember finding Jacob's marital arrangements – which included not only his two cousins, the sisters Leah and Rachel, but their maids as well – extremely confusing when I first heard it in Sunday school. No one explained the social structure of the time. It was the first I knew that bigamy had been perfectly acceptable in certain eras and locations. But I loved Jacob's passion and loyalty and perseverance, his willingness to put his head down and work for as long as it took to get what he wanted.

That stubborn addiction to honest toil can be found in congregations too – the groups that knit mitts and hold bake sales, or rip apart the old furnace room and turn it into a Sunday school classroom – and keep their church open.

Finally, having made Laban wealthy by his skilled farming, Jacob tricks him as well, and sets out for his own ancestral home with his accumulated wives, concubines, children, and flocks. His father-in-law pursues him. There is direct talk. One wonders if it is the first straight speaking these two schemers have ever managed.

Finally they come to an agreement. Laban pronounces these stern phrases – the first of which we have sentimentally appropriated for a thousand evening campfires, and the rest which we have largely banished from memory: "The Lord watch between you and me, when we are absent one from the other. If you ill-treat my daughters… though no one else is with us, remember that God is a witness…"

But Jacob is not as confident about achieving a truce with Esau, whom he has cheated twice. Typically, he plans ahead, sending a messenger with a carefully worded message of reconciliation. Esau responds by mustering 400 men to meet his brother Jacob.

Jacob is terrified. He pleads with God for deliverance. He sends an impressive array of goats, cattle, sheep, camels, and donkeys as a peace offering to his brother. And he divides his people and animals into two companies, so they won't all be killed at once. He takes one contingent across a ford at the Jabbock River, but he himself returns the same night to his camp on the far side of the river.

Alone that night, he is joined by a man, and they wrestle until daybreak.

This part of the Jacob story seems especially analogous to the Christian church today. Picture the scene.

Endless darkness, and the grunting of two weary opponents, each unable to subdue the other. Finally the stranger dislocates Jacob's hip and demands to be released, "for the day is breaking." Jacob catches on, at last, that the "man" may be more than a man. Ever with an eye on the main chance, he demands a blessing. Instead the stranger asks his name, and Jacob tells him.

"You shall no longer be called Jacob," says the being, "but Israel, for you have striven with God and with humans and prevailed."

Being able to name something confers power. Jacob pleads for the stranger's name but is refused. This is not surprising, since this stranger clearly wishes neither to be seen, nor to give up power. He does, however, bestow the blessing Jacob longs for, and Jacob realizes he has been struggling with God.

As the sun rises, Jacob limps away, wounded but alive – a miracle, considering the nature of his opponent. The Jacob we knew is gone. Instead, his name is Israel. He will this day will be reconciled with his brother Esau. And before he dies, many chapters in Genesis later, he will pass on his blessing to all twelve of his sons.

Scholars tell us this story may have grown out of an ancient tradition that rivers are guarded by supernatural beings. In an earlier version, the Jacob figure may have encountered the *genius loci*, the spirit of the place itself.

But the crucial point for the Christian church, hungry in a secular age for good news, is that blessing. It must have been very powerful – Jacob knew the moment it was given that it was God who had embraced and wounded and renamed him.

What is the church's blessing today? What is our wound? How can we who live within the church find the strength to hold on to our adversary in the darkness, until we too receive our blessing?

The long night of change seems endless, and we cannot discern the way ahead. At times, we seem on the verge of losing all we cherish – even our collective life. Why is God struggling with us, changing us, this way? What is this new identity God is giving us? Will we be able, like Jacob, to walk with our limp, to be reconciled with those we have wronged, and to bless generations to come?

Jacob's story assures us that we will.

More than we can see

Jacob has other visions in which he encounters the reality of God – although not, we assume, with as much sweat. These experiences place him securely in the line of what Marcus Borg, in *Meeting Jesus Again for the First Time*, calls "spirit persons."[1] We might call them shamans: people who are able to mediate the sacred to others, who are somehow able to look on the face of God and emerge unscathed. Moses was one, says Borg. So was Jesus, the one whose experience of God is so intimate and real and ongoing that he could call God *Abba*. Papa.

In some traditions – Celtic for example – shamans or spirit people change shape and travel to other worlds. In aboriginal cultures they embark on vision quests – like Jesus in the wilderness, or Jacob alone by the river Jabbock – opening themselves to a reality we in the modern world are only now beginning to rediscover. Borg puts it this way:

The experience of spirit persons presupposes an understanding of reality very different from the dominant image of reality in the modern Western world. The modern world view, derived from the Enlightenment, sees reality in material terms, as constituted by the world of matter and energy within the space-time continuum. The experience of spirit persons suggests there is more to reality than this – that there is, in addition to the tangible world of our ordinary experience, a nonmaterial level of reality, actual even through nonmaterial, and charged with energy and power. The modern worldview is one-dimensional; the worldview of spirit persons is multidimensional.[2]

People today – like those women getting ready to braid sweet grass, wanting to pray, and knowing that prayer and Creation are related – are eager for this multidimensional awareness.

The elements of Jacob's blessing

We, the authors of this book, are convinced that a strong belief in what Borg calls the "nonmaterial level of reality…charged with energy and power" will be a major aspect of the church that is coming into being. **Blessing 5, Partners in Spirituality,** describes our search for a more mystical spirituality, one that allows us to take dreams and inner promptings seriously. **Blessing 4, The Whole Person**, makes concrete this yearning to be in touch with mystery we do not understand, and to bring the ancient alliance of faith and healing back together.

Of course, because this new church comes into being in fits and starts, we get only glimpses. Some congregations offer Therapeutic and Healing Touch. Here and there, church members are building – and walking – labyrinths. They are having their heads anointed with oil. And above all they are praying for each other as if they mean it, as if God really can do miracles. Talking to God. Badgering God. Wrestling with God.

A previous encounter

On his way to his fateful meeting with Rachel, Jacob stops at a place called Haran. He sleeps with his head on a powerful stone, a rock that must have been replete (like the water of the Jabbock River) with the lively spirit of the place. There Jacob has an extravagant dream in which God promises him many descendants: "All the families of the earth shall be blessed in you and your offspring."

Jacob gets up early and constructs a pillar, with that strong, living stone at the top. He anoints the stone with oil and makes his promise, in turn, to God. If God will accompany him, and give him "bread to eat and clothing to wear," then the LORD will be his God, and "of all that you give me I will surely give one tenth to you."

In that promise, we find the roots of our commitment to both justice and stewardship. **Blessing 2, Commitment to a Cause** and **Blessing 10,**

Encountering the Economy, are about bread to eat together, commitment to God ("one tenth to you," Jacob promised), and stewardship for all that God gives us.

Before the light returns

Jacob's encounter with the stranger at the Jabbock River, whom he later decides is God, took place entirely in darkness. Jacob cannot see what's happening; he can only assume that the sun will rise as usual.

The household I inhabit is supremely normal in every way except one. Both of us are intensely involved with the church. My husband is an ordained minister and regional staff person; I work for our denominational magazine. This leads to intense discussions about our church's future. Only this morning at breakfast I heard myself declaiming, wailing in fact, that we would never see the Promised Land, that the shape of the new church-to-be would not become clear in our lifetime. It is as difficult for us to see what we are struggling with as it was for Jacob.

Perhaps I had not yet had sufficient coffee.

But those who like certainty find this period, when Christendom-as-it-was slowly comes apart,[3] especially difficult. It's not that our household is committed to the triumphalism that has affected the church ever since Emperor Constantine made Christianity his official religion in the 4th century. It's just that we can't see what's happening.

I have to remind myself that Jacob had his clearest encounters with God in the dark, at Bethel and at the edge of the River Jabbock. In both cases he must have been propelled by fear, either running from his brother Esau's fury, or – he thought – moving hesitantly towards it. He was, in fact, a refugee, first from his brother and then from his father-in-law, his uncle Laban.

That's our story too. And author Bruce McLeod points out:

What distinguishes us from refugees is that they hang on through darkness that we, with more choices open to us, try to tame. They don't have the option to change the subject, pretend they'll deal with it next week, or hurry off to deal with more pressing matters… In fact it is through those people who wait steadfastly in the dark and prevail that light breaks through and shines.[4]

Perhaps, in the darkness of uncertainty, as a church and as church members, we will learn some strengths we didn't need before. I – over my morning coffee – will learn patience, calmness in the face of the unknown.

These flights from the old ways are long and slow. The night of wrestling must have seemed forever to Jacob. So must Paul's wait in prison, in Rome, isolated from the churches he had founded and loved. The days before his excommunication, the days of uncertainty, must have been seemed endless for Martin Luther.

Now that a new reformation is at hand – now that we are discovering that we are not in charge of the universe, for example, but only one of the creatures God made (see **Blessing 3, In Touch with Mystery**) – our limping passage towards newness may seem to last forever.

Jacob's welcome home

But we can take heart. Our studies of Jacob focus so often on that struggle by the river that we forget to note what happens the day after.

Jacob, frightened into anguished choice, splits his people into two companies in the hope that some might survive.

Esau approaches with 400 men.

Jacob arranges his family so that those he values most are to the rear, the safest area: the two maids and their children in front, and then Leah and her children, and finally Rachel and her son Joseph. But Jacob reveals his new humility as he places himself in front of all of them, and prostrates himself on the ground seven times.

Instead of seeking revenge, Esau runs to meet him and embraces him, and falls on his neck and kisses him, and they weep.

It's a lovely passage. The one who was lost has been found; the one who was missing has returned. It anticipates a similar reconciliation, later in scripture, when Jesus tells the parable of the prodigal son. To go home, says this part of the Jacob story, you must first be reconciled with your brother.

In the North American church, 500 years after Columbus, we too have brothers and sisters with whom we must be reconciled. Before we can find ourselves at home again as a church, we must make our peace with the aboriginal people whose inheritance we usurped just as Jacob stole Esau's birthright. **Blessing 5, Partners in Spirituality**, attempts to show the beginnings of this reconciliation.

One way of interpreting the scene by the river suggests that Jacob has wrestled with what, in Carl Jung's term, is called his "shadow" – all that he has failed to acknowledge about himself. At daybreak, he is more whole and complete than he has ever been, no longer hiding anything from himself or others.

For the Christian church in North America to wrestle with its collective sin is very hard and very necessary. The notion that we have the only way to salvation – that Christians know best – was institutionalized in Canada in our Indian residential schools. But the anguish created by taking children from their families and trying to mold them into an alien culture is slowly forcing itself into the nation's consciousness. It has led this nation's four historic mission churches – Roman Catholic, Anglican, United and Presbyterian – into a powerful confrontation with themselves.

In the same way, the churches of Christendom, with varying energy, are coming to grips with their blindness in terms of their Jewish brothers and sisters. Some members are slowly beginning to read the gospels in conscious knowledge that Jesus was a Jew, seeking to clear their heads and hearts of the anti-Semitism implied in certain interpretations of Christian scripture. And they are studying, learning – in the words of one paper now under discussion – how

Early in its history, the Church came to see itself as the new Israel, displacing and superseding the Jews as the People of God. It took this stance from a narrow interpre-

tation of its Gospels and especially from its passion narratives. The Jews were portrayed as enemies of Jesus, blind to his fulfillment of God's promises, stubbornly rebellious in the face of his work, and responsible for his death... Due to the lack of theological guidance, there is still the danger of anti-Judaic teaching and preaching in our church.[5]

When less will be more

We are beginning to know ourselves, as churches, a little better than we used to. Out of that hard-won self-knowledge and painful wrestling may come a new identity: a new church, closer to the earth, more committed to justice, and (the two are related) much more attuned to its own scripture.

We will have lost something, of course, we Christians. Like Jacob, our self-centeredness will be replaced with humility. We may limp a little; we will certainly walk more slowly, more carefully. But we will be more whole.

It's hard to give up the notion — long held by many, however erroneous — that we are the only ones with the plan for salvation; we know the only road to God. We may well wonder if we are still needed. What is the church for, some people wonder, if it is not to show the only true way, the way that we alone understand?

Perhaps part of what the church is for — as author Francis Fukuyama suggested in an article in *The Atlantic Monthly*[6] — is to hold on to ritual and cultural tradition in a world filled with transience. It will help our children examine and articulate their values, "using religion as a language with which to express their moral beliefs."

But there's much more, and it can already be dimly observed. Like the Kingdom of God, the new church to come is both here and not-yet-here. We can see bits of it when people gather in church seeking the friendship of Jesus.

We can see it when people name wrongs — as the Christian church has many times done bravely — distinguishing itself from a too-complacent culture. We see it at Christmas gatherings when children and adults live inside the biblical story and make it real and incarnate for all of us. We see it when we reach out for each other, long-lost, like Esau and Jacob, and kiss, and weep.

And we see it most of all when we wrestle willingly with all that is mysterious and new and scary, to discover in the end that it is God who embraces us and gives us a new name, showing us our well-earned wounds and making us whole.

Commitment to a Cause

CHRISTOPHER WHITE

Then Jacob made a vow saying, "If God will be with me, and
will keep me in this way that I go,
and will give me bread to eat and clothing to wear,
so that I may come again to my father's house in peace, then
the LORD shall be my God."
Genesis 28:20–21

My friends Tom and Frank are tenors in the community choir directed by my wife, Wendy. They are terrific choir members, prompt, always at rehearsal. They are helpful, enthusiastic, and reliable. When we first attempted Handel's *Messiah,* they came to all the extra practices, were happy to set up the church before the concert, and stayed to clean up afterward.

They're just the type of people that you wish were in your church. In fact, they don't go to any church at all. But they used to. A local congregation used to benefit from the enthusiasm and loyalty that they now demonstrate in their choir. But they drifted away. "It just didn't seem to mean anything," Frank shrugged, when I asked him about the change.

Tom agreed: "We sang in the church choir, too. And we were on all sorts of committees. But at some point, all the effort we were putting in didn't make sense in our lives."

"We had questions and concerns," Frank picked up the explanation. "But they weren't being addressed. We felt we were making more of a contribution in other places–"

"–like this choir," Tom interrupted. "Or at the cottage."

Frank finished: "So we left."

The fact two people with this attitude are elsewhere Sunday mornings speaks volumes about the challenges that lie ahead for congregations.

A biblical precedent

But in the challenge, there's also hope. Because one of our ancestors in the faith, Jacob, eventually the father of the twelve tribes of Israel, also drifted away.

The whole story of Jacob deals with ambiguity, complexity, and contradiction. It parallels the current situations facing our congregations.

Jacob, like us, lived in a time of great fluidity. He constantly had to adapt. The nomadic world into which he was born was very different from the world where his son Joseph would eventually rule in Egypt. Jacob's strength lay in his willingness to learn from and to experience God wherever he was. That is why this story is so apt for us.

For years, Jacob seemed headed for juvenile court – or worse. He cheated his brother, at least twice. He deceived his own father on what was supposed to be Isaac's deathbed. He was so afraid of vengeance that he fled from his family. And yet, lying on the ground, exhausted from his flight, he encountered God, and the two of them made a long-term covenant with each other.

That covenant with God sustained him through 14 years of labor for his father-in-law Laban, as compensation for his two wives, Leah and Rachel. It gave him the courage, eventually, to pack up and move back to his homeland, and to face the anger of his brother Esau.

A church stuck in its rut

In most denominations, congregational life is based more in history than present reality. These congregations still expect to function in a world that doesn't exist anymore – a world where women stay home, men work nine to five, and both have lots of disposable time to volunteer to their church.

Look at your congregation's organizational structure. You probably have some type of central board, supported by a variety of committees; the most typical ones are Worship, Finance (or Stewardship), Property, and Christian Education.

Now think about the reaction last year, when the nominating committee sought people to replace outgoing committee members. When the vacancies were announced, did the phone ring off the hook? Did people cluster around after church in order to secure these prized positions? Or was there a dead silence, followed by averted eyes, and unreturned phone calls?

Are the key people on your committees, and the teachers in your Sunday school, recent arrivals? Or are they people who have been doing these tasks for 20 years because no one else is willing to?

More specifically, look at your turkey supper. I doubt if there's a mainline church across North America that does not have some kind of annual turkey supper, beef barbecue, or lobster boil. Personally, I love these dinners. I actually enjoy helping to cut turnips, pour coffee, wash dishes, and visit with everybody. In our church, the nursery becomes the pie room. It's my favorite room. Acres of pumpkin and lemon meringue pie blanket the tables, waiting to feed the hungry hordes.

The turkey supper is invariably staffed by the "ladies" of the church. Year after year, the same group of devoted women organize the whole event. Most of these women come from the pre-war generation. After World War II, they and their husbands moved to our community, bought land provided for veterans, built houses, and raised their families. Most are now in their 70s. They were raised in a world where the church was one of the centers of life; most of them did not work outside of the home.

Their daughters and sons, however, do not bake pies. Bake? They react to the request as if being asked to engage in an unknown and slightly perverse act. Who has time to bake? They catch the commuter train to town at 7:00 a.m.; they get home after 6:00 p.m. They drive the kids to their activities, make supper, do housework, and get ready to do it all over again the next morning. If they stay home at all, it's for maternity leave, or possibly a few years away from their careers until the children are in school. Their lemon meringue pies come from chain stores and require defrosting. If they do bake, it's a big deal, a special treat for their family, not for the church supper.

When the women who bake the pies and coordinate turkey suppers are simply too old to keep the effort going, these events could well disappear forever. Reality will have caught up with congregational life.

Meantime, the younger families are frightened about the future, and carrying heavy debt loads. They want the best for their children. So they have enrolled those kids in swimming, skating, ballet, karate, gymnastics, and every type of music known. That is what comes first, not the church. The church, frankly, is not that important for many of them. They like coming Christmas Eve. They enjoy a children's pageant. They say they want the values that the church has to offer. But they feel as if they pass through some kind of a time warp when they walk through the church doors. The church they encounter still operates in the same way as it did in their parents' and grandparents' world, a world that no longer exists for them.

The new economic reality

To comprehend the new world that congregations must now live in, we need to understand what is happening in the global world of which the church is a part.

Author George Soros describes the enormous volatility of the world economy. Job security is a historic memory; a "survival of the fittest" mentality affects almost everyone.

A recent phone-in program on Toronto radio station CFRB focused on a strike by educational workers. One caller said that he could lose his job anytime; if he didn't have job security, he didn't see why educational workers should. The program's host, Michael Coren, well known for right-wing views, paused for a moment, and then asked, "Why would you want it to be as bad for others as it is for you?"

There was a startled silence. Finally the caller replied, "I can't answer that."

But the caller's attitude will hardly surprise anyone today. As George Soros points out, in his book *The Crisis of Global Capitalism,* we live in a time ruled by the free flight of capital. "Market fundamentalism," he charges, has "rendered the global capitalist system unsound and unstable."[1] His thesis is supported by others. *Business Week* writers William Wolman and Anne Colamosca call the impact of the flight of capital, "the betrayal of the American worker."[2] Global volatility, they say, has led to a time when "Family incomes have fallen…jobs have become less secure…and the net wealth of the typical middle class family has also fallen."[3]

In his examination of the Canadian economy, pollster Angus Reid wrote:

It's a harsh economy when people are forced to take on two or three jobs, often without benefits, to make ends meet. The movement to part-time, flexible work is swamping the job market. We're talking about the creation of a new "servant class," whose main role will be to attend to the personal needs of the wealthiest 20% of the population. This is the 20% that advises ordinary people to make themselves "flexible" in the workplace.[4]

The global economy, the loss of loyalty, the impact of the free movement of capital, have become seismic changes in people's lives. We need to ask how the church has responded.

Responding to reality

Sadly, we have been more reactive then proactive.

Our people experience organizational change every day, except at church. In my own denomination, the governing structure has not substantially changed since it was founded in 1925 as the merger of the Methodist, Congregational, Union, and most of the Presbyterian Churches of Canada. What other organization can make such a claim?

My denomination, the United Church of Canada, is divided into regional conferences, and smaller regional units called presbyteries. The boundaries of those regional bodies were originally set up along railway lines, so clergy and laity could more easily travel to meetings. Railways today fall a distant third behind cars and airplanes as a means of travel – and instant communication by phone, fax, and e-mail often makes travel itself unnecessary. But those boundaries are still held as inviolate as if they had been divinely ordained.

Every time a major proposal comes forward to restructure and reorganize the church, it is defeated at either the regional or national levels. People comfortable with the way things are resist change with the tenacity of barnacles on the hull of a sinking ship. Yet change is being forced upon us as denominational finances dwindle. Restructuring is happening – not voluntarily, but out of sheer necessity – in the "higher" courts of the church.

But the real challenge will lie in how local congregations reorganize and adapt their structures at the local level. This is more than moving the deck chairs around on the *Titanic*. How we operate must make sense. We urgently need to address the central issue: how does the Christian story answer the fundamental life questions, at this time in our history, for a stressed-out and frightened people?

Some respond that we must become user friendly, use the tools of the time. Bring in theatre-style worship, play contemporary music, eliminate traditional symbols… That's what the megachurches do, isn't it?

But there is danger there. That format will have no staying power, if it arises only out of the culture of the moment. And when that culture changes – as surely it will – our congregations will be left without substance, unable even to remember the questions they were trying to answer with their new techniques, let alone the answers offered by the ancient wisdom of the church.

Still others believe that the answer lies in language and theology. Traditional concepts like the Resurrection no longer make sense to the modern mind, they claim. Much of Christian theology arose out of a pre-scientific age, when the heavens were thought to be in the sky above the earth. Thus, the very tenets of the faith need to be changed.

This argument falls into the same trap as the first. It attempts to re-shape the church to make it accessible for this particular moment in history, to adapt it solely to this generation's perceptions of truth.

I'm not suggesting that theology and worship can't and shouldn't change. God is revealed in new ways all the time. But it does mean that we should be careful not to throw Jesus out with the bath water.

Gourmet cooking for 300

As I write, we have recently lost two families from our congregation. They have drifted into Sunday sports and other activities that they feel are more valuable for their children than church. They're not taking the easy way out. As one mother commented, "My daughter's soccer team makes a lot more demands on her, and on us, than the church did."

But there are others who, like Jacob, move in the opposite direction.

Stevie Cameron is an active member of St. Andrew's Presbyterian Church in downtown Toronto, a historic church that recalls the glories of the city's history. For years, church was not a part of Stevie Cameron's life. But then her life began to change, her friends started to die, and she discovered that she was missing a community of faith to help her get through these transitions. So she started to "church shop." At St. Andrew's she found a sense of belonging. She loved the music, and was challenged by the sermons.

But she was not content just to sit in on Sundays. If she was going to attend, she told me in an interview, she needed to be truly committed.

About this time, people in Toronto were growing concerned about the homeless on their streets. People were dying of exposure and hunger in the wealthiest city in Canada, in a country that the United Nations rates the best place to live on earth. Clearly, it's not the "best place" for *all* Canadian citizens.

Toronto churches responded with the "Out of the Cold" Program. It was based on the biblical premise that the church is called to provide for the poor and dispossessed. John's gospel says, "Feed my sheep!" Homeless folks are fed dinner and given shelter for the night. Cameron was one of those who urged St. Andrew's to join this important ministry.

Not surprisingly, the governing bodies of the church had concerns. "What would it do to the church to have poor people sleeping in our basement?" they wondered.

And the obvious response came back: "What does it do to the church to have those people sleeping on our sidewalks?"

Stevie Cameron and her co-workers estimated that maybe 50 people would show up the first night. They prepared a meal of powdered soup, day-old donated muffins, and donuts. When they opened the church doors, almost 100 people crowded the steps, too many for the food prepared. A group of Catholic nuns arrived to help out and see how the volunteers were doing. They all shook their heads in dismay, opened their wallets, pooled their resources, and ordered pizzas.

That first night was an eye opener for Stevie. The food wasn't what she would want to eat, and she wasn't surprised that nobody else wanted it either. "Why should the poor get the leftovers of our tables," she wondered. "Why should they always get other people's castoffs?"

That night she determined to do something about it. By coincidence, she knew how to prepare food that is both appetizing and nutritious; she's a trained chef. In spite of an extremely busy journalistic schedule, Stevie decided that she would give the gift of her skill to the homeless. So she spent every Sunday night in the church basement preparing soups, stews, and casseroles for the people who would be fed the next day.

It was an incredible commitment, completed without resentment, and without having her arm twisted by the chair of some nominating committee. It was lived out of genuine, old-fashioned Christian love and faith.

The gift of community

The results of her living faith have been spectacular. Every Monday night 300 people crowd into that church basement, served by 250 volunteers. Business people and teachers, men and women, gladly give their time to participate in this taste of God's kingdom.

The project now receives free toiletries. Clean, dry socks and underwear are available. They have started a résumé service to help people find jobs. A health bus with nurses and three examining rooms arrives to deal with ailments. Clean thermal blankets and fresh pillow cases make the homeless visitors comfortable for the night.

St. Andrew's stands proudly in the heart of Toronto's theatre district, minutes from the high-rise financial emporiums of Bay Street, Canada's Wall Street Office towers, condominiums, and renovated lofts surround the church. It is a place of 24-hour busyness and complete anonymity. Nobody knows you on those streets and nobody particularly cares either.

But they know you at St. Andrew's. They know your name and your face and they care about you. It is a ministry that creates a visible impact in that downtown neighborhood.

But the impact is not simply on the people receiving these services. In some ways the greatest impact is reserved for those who serve.

"What does the church offer that no one else does?" I asked Cameron.

"Community," was her immediate reply.

Where else in our society can you find a place that provides an opportunity to serve your neighbor and find yourself at the same time? True intimacy is almost completely absent in our public life. We routinely ask each other the most dangerous question one human being can ask another: "How are you?" – knowing that they will not tell us, that we don't really want to know.

Except in church. There we do want to know. And we will truly listen to the answer.

That's the gift of community.

It can happen anywhere

But Stevie Cameron wasn't finished with her answer. "There's something about us that we have to change. Mainline churches simply don't demand enough of their people. We don't demand enough of their time, and we don't demand enough of their money."

She's right – but we have to demand the right sort of things. Too often, we beg their time and energy simply to maintain the institution. But we don't offer them mission. A recent *Maclean's* magazine article asserted that for most Canadians, the most important factor in their employment is not money or security, but a sense of doing something worthwhile. If they have a sense of mission, people will no longer experience committees and board work as time wasted – rather, they will welcome meetings as a means of developing strategies to carry out that mission.

Remember those turkey suppers I mentioned earlier? Since I began writing this chapter, something interesting happened. One Sunday, during worship, I told the story of Stevie Cameron and her "Out of the Cold" suppers. Soon people started donating tickets for customers of St. Vincent's Kitchen, a church run, dollar-a-meal restaurant in a neighboring community for those in need.

People caught a vision in Cameron's story, a sense of what a traditional turkey dinner could become. But it goes beyond that. Helen, a matriarch of our church, asked me how many people St. Vincent's feeds each night.

"About 200 adults and over a dozen children," I replied.

"We can't give away that many tickets," she said. Then she added, thoughtfully, "But we could put on a whole other dinner."

This is how God's Kingdom is built. Small gesture by small gesture. By people like Stevie. And Helen. And you.

COMMITMENT TO A CAUSE ✦ 41

Different folks

My father was raised in the great Depression. He has a tendency to snort derisively when I try to talk to him about the stress of our times. "I lived through a war," he says." I remember my best Christmas present being a real pair of winter boots. Real stress is no money, no work, and dodging bullets in a war where you could very well get killed."

We are not the first people to undergo difficult times. A very long way back, Jacob's ancestors were refugees, homeless people, transients with "no fixed address." Jacob's descendants were slaves, people whose lives had no value. That does not diminish our experience of dislocation, but it does put it into context.

Times change, and so do expectations. My Dad comes from a generation that is now in their 70s and 80s. Our future elders are the boomers, raised in relative abundance. Their experiences and my father's are dramatically different. The true test of the boomers' character will be their response to Stevie Cameron's clarion call, that our churches should ask a lot more from people.

Mainline churches generally don't expect a high level of commitment. We offer a buffet lifestyle: come on in and taste a morsel or so. We offer the sacraments to everyone who professes – by silence – a faith in Jesus. While there was a time when we got sticky about baptizing anyone, most of our churches would rather risk being too open than risk offending someone – even if that person hasn't been in church since their last child was "done." Splash and split is our policy.

Money? We won't talk about money. That might upset you. Volunteer your time? We won't pressure you, except in the vaguest, most unthreatening way possible.

In the immediate post-war years, this policy worked like a charm. But those years were an aberration in the history of the church. A confluence of factors led to an unprecedented burst of growth that the church realistically could never sustain. In my denomination, in the 1950s, we boasted that we were opening one new church, church hall, or manse every week. That growth placed impossible expectations on future generations.

World War II left, in its wake, a huge consumer demand. Not simply for consumer goods, but for peace and normality. Depression and war had seared the souls of a whole generation. More then anything else they wanted peace and prosperity, communities with churches in them as places to reinforce and support these values. This generation's children flooded into the church. But the boom went bust. The flood tide inevitably ebbed.

We are our history

Instead of comparing ourselves simply to the recent past, perhaps it is time to take a look at our longer history.

John Stephenson is the Chair of Theology and Biblical studies at the Eastern Pentecostal Bible College in Peterborough, Ontario. He is also completing his Th.D. at the Toronto School of Theology, through Wycliffe College. Stephenson has examined why denominations decline, by studying historic denominations in England. His conclusions are both fascinating and challenging.

To my surprise, he told me that the Pentecostal church was in decline. For years, those of us in the mainline churches have been told of growth in conservative congregations. By implication, if we adopted their methods and theology, we too would grow. "Not so," Stephenson said when I interviewed him. "The Pentecostal church declined by 5 percent between 1993–1996." They hoped to plant 400 churches across Canada in what they called a "Decade of Destiny." In fact, they planted just 89 – still quite an accomplishment, but far short of their target. The very same factors that led to decline in the mainline churches are now starting to affect Pentecostal bodies.

Prof. Stephenson divides decline into Macro and Micro factors.

Macro reasons for decline

1. *War.* People don't flock to churches during wartime. Indeed, the opposite is true. Leadership is lost, and people are too preoccupied with the impact of war to pay much attention to church.
2. *Internal strife.* Struggles in a church's own governance, and divisive strife over issues, filter down to the local congregation and cause decline. Some individual congregations may still grow, but in general the denominational difficulties will start manifesting themselves.
3. *Group decline.* When a denomination as a collective group begins to decline, this begins to affect the mindset of all members of all churches.
4. *Competition.* Congregations find themselves in a battle to maintain "market share" and wind up competing for an ever-dwindling number of people.
5. *Loss of distinctives.* This is, Stephenson says, the most critical factor in decline. Distinctives are those elements of identity that set one denomination apart from other denominations. Distinctives define us as churches. When we lose our distinctives, then we lose identity. Robert Curry, another church writer, believes that the drive to structural union among denominations reflects, and results from, decline; it implies that those denominations have already lost their distinctiveness. That will not be a popular thought in my own denomination, the United Church of Canada. But there is some truth to it. Our Church Union, in 1925, gave us a uniquely Canadian identity. But the Methodists who were the biggest denomination entering into that union were already losing numbers. They had had several mergers in the previous century, largely driven by declining attendance. Between 1916–1926, for example, Methodists in the U.S. declined 12.3 percent. Other mainline churches experienced similar losses. Attendance in the 1920s was roughly proportionate to today's.

Micro reasons for decline

1. *Long-term economic difficulties.* Churches rally in the short term, but in a long-term economic shift they lose members and even hope. In 1860 the economy of the English town of Congleton collapsed when Free Trade in silk was introduced with France. The church grew for three to four years, as people turned to it for help and consolation, but then began a decline from which it never recovered. This has profound consequences for us in Canada, where, for the first time in 150 years, the middle class is shrinking rapidly.

2. *Failure to adjust to local change.* When populations in a community change, churches often act as though nothing is different. Churches must constantly adapt to new realities.

3. *Restricted lay leadership.* If leadership becomes centralized in one or two lay persons, rather than shared by many, conflict and decline inevitably follow.

4. *Authoritarian pastoral leadership.* Power must be shared by those at the center.

5. *Failure to differentiate.* Loss of a church's unique identity in a community means decline. Bland does not attract people.

6. *Debt.* Major debt strangles growth and preoccupies the church above everything else. It can literally kill a church.

A Canadian paradigm

These factors can be seen at work in many areas, not just in churches.

Eaton's, a Canadian department store, was a national success story. Starting in the late 19th century with one store in downtown Toronto, Eaton's expanded to become Canada's national retail chain. Between its stores and its catalogues, *everyone* shopped at Eaton's. Then the retail climate changed, but Eaton's kept operating the way it always had. Eaton's kept believing that if it just did the same things that had worked in the past, things would turn around. But Wal-Mart and other "big box retailers" with their warehouse stores and discounted prices had changed the game. Eaton's had to seek bankruptcy protection. As I write this chapter, Eaton's is bankrupt and in the process of being dismantled.

The mainline churches are the Eaton's of Canadian religion. The churches acted just as Eaton's did. They failed to recognize irrevocable changes in society, Sunday was now just like Saturday, and Saturday was like every other day of the week. The churches failed to appreciate how the need for two incomes affected families. Their economic analysis failed to take into account the declining purchasing power of the average family.

Traditionally, the mainline church has always seen itself as part of the individual's life, but not fundamental to that person's core identity. Like the curling club or the children's gymnastics, we have been content to be *part* of people's lives.

To thrive in the future, we have to shift our focus. Because if we are only a minor part of life, then we get minor commitment and a minor church. Professor John Stephenson firmly believes that the church, whether Pentecostal or liberal mainline, can have a vibrant future. But it will depend on three critical elements.

1. A church has a strong sense of its own identity and what makes it distinctive.
2. It has a powerful sense of mission to the world.
3. There is a strong spiritual dynamic, with prayer at the center.

The good news is that people are ready for this change. They are looking for something meaningful to base their lives upon, a way of life, a true community.

The greatest strength of my denomination in the past has been its ability to be open, to question the very tenets of our faith and to invite others to join us on that quest. Yet I believe that it is possible to combine liberal exploration with traditional conservative church commitment. I believe it because I see it all the time in my own congregation. People have come back to church and are there almost every week, because if they don't go, they miss it. They are people who choose to be defined by their faith. And they are not just in my church, they are in yours as well.

If we do our jobs right, a lot more of them will be just like that.

In Touch with Mystery

DONNA SINCLAIR

"...I am the God of Bethel, where you anointed a pillar and made a vow to me. Now leave this land at once and return to the land of your birth."
Genesis 31:13

Then Jonah prayed to the LORD his God from the belly of the fish, saying,
"I called to the LORD out of my distress,
and he answered me...
Jonah began to go into the city... And he cried out,
"Forty days more, and Nineveh shall be overthrown!" And the people of Nineveh believed God;
they proclaimed a fast, and everyone,
great and small put on sackcloth.
When God saw what they did, how they turned from their evil ways, God changed God's mind about the calamity that God had said would be brought upon them.
And God did not do it.
Jonah 2:1–2a and 3:4–5, 10 (paraphrase)

I live in a small city on the shores of a big lake in northern Ontario. Born and raised nearby, both of us – my husband and I – worked elsewhere, but came home to the north as soon as we could. Like salmon or geese or any other creature of instinct, we knew where we belonged. We've lived here for the last 20 years.

We like to walk the shoreline in the mornings.

It's changed in the last decade, and especially in the last few years. After years of turning their backs on it, the city's inhabitants began to cherish their waterfront. Landscapers were hired, paths laid so the beaches were accessible, trees planted, gardens dug. Several years after that, when the gardens showed signs of neglect, a few enterprising volunteers began to clean them up.

It's the beginning of a lovely story. The more they weeded, the more volunteers appeared. Now there are 250 of them, maintaining the beds, mulching, weeding, planting, learning – delighting in touching the earth.

I believe these gardeners are a powerful symbol of a new spirituality that is appearing. It's not that they would name themselves as prophets. They're just making the city where they live clean and beautiful. Loving it.

The earth is great need of such love. In every corner of the continent, North Americans have only to look around – at our few remaining old-growth forests, casually threatened; at a land and water often tainted with pesticides or industrial wastes; at plans for new hydro megaprojects – to see and hear the warning splash of Jonah's mighty fish.

We might almost imagine the prophet himself, striding up the shore, fresh from the belly of the whale. "Forty days more," Jonah might thunder, as he does in scripture, "and Nineveh [or North America] shall be overwhelmed."

I believe at some level, those gardeners hear him. So do the activists who camp out, when necessary, in Temagami's old-growth forest just north of here. So, for another example, do the Innu of *Nitassinan* (Labrador) who oppose another round of flooded land and methylmercury-poisoned water in the name of electricity for sale.

Even as governments in some jurisdictions whittle away at environmental regulation, people all over this continent struggle to pay attention to the land. Alert citizens ban chemicals from their lawns, seek out heritage seeds, and compost as if their lives depended on it.

I believe these actions are holy and mysterious. I believe these people want to heal the earth.

Eighty percent absent

There is a new vision for the Christian church in these gardeners and in Jonah's story. It has to do with those people who are not in church, as well as those who are – especially the young ones, aged 20 to 29. According to sociologist Reginald Bibby in *Unknown Gods: The Ongoing Story of Religion in Canada*, only 14 percent of those young people aged 20–24 attend church weekly, and only 6 percent of those aged 25–29.[1]

Those who avoid church have their reasons. It may be apathy, or lethargy – or it may be more significant. When our oldest son set off to university, for instance, he returned home the first Thanksgiving holiday filled with delight at the new world he had entered. Already he was busy with a group that was setting up a recycling program at his residence. "I'll come back to church," he assured me that weekend, "when it takes the environmental crisis as seriously as human rights. What's the point of making the world safe for oppressed people if there is no world left for them to live in?"

Progress has been made since he and I had that conversation several years ago. Many congregations are involved in recycling and local cleanups. Hundreds of thousands of Canadian churchgoers have signed a petition calling for stronger government effort on global warming. And most denominations produce serious environmental statements at their General Synods or Councils or Assemblies.

Still, not that many of my generation's children sit in church pews on Sunday. A considerable number of them were (or are) sitting at Temagami or Clayoquot Sound instead, protecting the forest. It may be that the church has missed some pieces of an important equation.

Denying the earth's pain

One piece may be that – along with everyone else – the churches are still denying the pain of the earth. If we, as a people, allow ourselves to feel our connection with it, we have to feel its anguish. And few of us are good at sitting with pain. We pretend it is not there, that nothing is wrong, that it is not necessary to lament when fishers' nets are empty of cod, when hillsides stand bare, when caribou have difficulty calving.

But we, above all, should be wailing in mourning. It is our work, as people of faith, to mourn the death of those who once lived, all the small creatures that have lost their habitat, all the land that has lost its goodness. We are the ones who – knowing that we are escorted by a loving God through the hard valley of the shadow – can find the strength to walk it.

And we are the ones who have been given the words with which to mourn. From Lamentations, for example:

The joy of our hearts has ceased;
our dancing has been turned to mourning.
The crown has fallen from our head;
woe to us, for we have sinned! (Lamentations 5:15–16)

Instead of taking these words as our own, we often numb ourselves into believing that somehow global warming is not happening; that we are not inextricably connected with one another and with the earth.

Deep down, I believe, people know that they have allowed themselves to be split away from nature. That's why many feel dry spiritually, and why, if they visit a spiritual director, they may be advised to walk in the bush. It's why we garden. Few of our songs and poems are about the land; we dare not allow ourselves to feel our love for it, because – as the family farm is sold to hungry agribusiness, as the smog smears the streets – we fear its pain.

At some level, though, we know the Creator inhabits trees and rocks as well as people. Like Jacob dreaming on that powerful stone, we learned it, intuitively, during childhood summers around a campfire clearing where the spruce thrust dark spikes towards the icy stars, and we trembled at the majesty of God.

Disconnected theology

Another reason we deny our relationship with the earth is that many of us subscribe to a theology that suggests we don't have one. That as humans we are not connected in any deep way to Creation around us. That – to quote the apostle Paul out of context – we are "in this world but not of it."

But that, says theologian Rosemary Radford Ruether in *Gaia and God: An Ecofeminist Theology of Earth Healing*, is to forget our own history as covenantal people. We are people who make promises to God (as Jacob did, anointing the stone) and we are accountable to God for the safety of the world we inhabit:

A covenantal vision of the relation of humans to other life forms acknowledges the special place of humans in this relationship as caretakers, caretakers who did not create and do not absolutely own the rest of life, but are ultimately accountable for its welfare to the true source of life, God. This covenantal vision recognizes that humans and other life forms are part of one family, sisters and brothers in one community of interdependence.[2]

Such a vision, says Ruether, is to be found within our own scripture. "The Christian tradition is one of those communities of accountability that has profoundly valuable themes for ecological spirituality and practice."

Christianity, she admits, bears "significant responsibility for the legacy of domination of women and nature. But...its liberating potential should not be disregarded."[3]

Once upon a time, Christian churches took very seriously our connection with the earth. St. Francis and his Little Brothers, particularly, come to mind. In many ways, we have only to look to our ancestors for wisdom that the church of today, as congregation or denomination, could use.

The ancient wisdom of tribal people

I was interviewing an Ojibway spiritual elder whose counsel I have often sought. In the course of our conversation – which was about dreams and how they are regarded in a tribal culture like his own – he gently pointed out that "all of us were tribal people once. But some of us have lost their way."

He meant that to be comforting. But his words echoed in my mind for days. I had grown up in northern Ontario. The heart-stopping grace of a white pine, of granite carved by millennia and glaciers – I could never find words to express my sense of belonging to them. My friend seemed to say that this could never be mine again, that my people had given up that relationship centuries ago for the sake of Empire.

And then, a few years later, I stumbled across my own ancestors, the Celts – or rather they stumbled into me. I began to hear their music and legends everywhere: on the radio, on stage, in theatres. The ancient peoples of Ireland and Scotland and Wales did not have a Christianity that drew sharp lines between God and earth, humans and other creatures. Their own deep love of the earth had been preserved when the Goths stormed Rome and the Roman legions and priests were called back to defend the imperial capital.

Left to their own devices, and influenced by the Eastern monastic tradition of the desert fathers, the Celts proceeded to develop a faith that, in the words of Celtic scholar Esther de Waal,

came out of a rural people, a hierarchical tribal-based society in which personal relationships were of paramount importance – not only relationships between people, but relationships with wild creatures and material things, and not the least, between this world and the next. It came out of a people who were not afraid to carry over their earlier pagan pre-Christian beliefs into Christianity and fuse the old with the new. [4]

I felt that I had found my home, a religion that didn't make me feel sad or guilty for loving trees and rocks and water. In fact, we had long been singing of this tradition in church: "All things bright and beautiful," for example. Or, "I bind unto myself today the virtues of the sunlit heaven" – lovely words attributed to St. Patrick.

Here was a faith that respected the rest of the creatures as much as humans. Witness this Celtic prayer to be said while milking the cows:

Come, Mary, and milk my cow;
Come, Bride, and encompass her;
Come Columba the benign
And twine thine arm around my cow.[5]

Contrast that picture, of Christian saints with their arms around the cow, with a modern feedlot where animals may stand knee-deep in manure. Or with a turkey barn, birds bred so heavy-breasted they cannot walk.

Or keep this prayer in mind, one day when you're caught in a traffic jam:

O son of the living God, old eternal King, I desire a hidden hut in the wilderness that
   it may be my home.
A narrow little blue stream beside it and a clear pool for the washing away of sin
   through the grace of the Holy Ghost.
A lovely wood close about it on every side, to nurse the birds with all sorts of voices and
   to hide them with its shelter...[6]

My own sudden yearning – it's almost an ache within me – for this contemplative picture makes me believe that there is room for a church more mystical than the one we have now. Such a church would be capable of calling home to it those young people who are carefully mapping and guarding ancient trees, or handing out information about global warming. Such a church would cherish those times when its members break the artificial boundaries (sometimes created by Christianity itself) between humans and nature. This is a church that could shelter environmentalists and poets, because, as a body, it would cherish the earth and mystery. It would feed the spiritual hunger of the age.

Angels everywhere but in church

In our mass media, angels are everywhere. There are books about them. Television programs, like *Touched by an Angel*. And movies, like *City of Angels*, the gentle story of an immortal one who falls to earth and finds the heaven that is here.

This interest in angels reveals the spiritual dryness of our time. People yearn for the boundaries between heaven and earth to be transformed and transfigured. The Celts – large numbers of whom settled in North America, and whose legacy still lingers – encountered angels everywhere.

And so do many today. They see angels by sickbeds and as people are dying. They are saved from traffic accidents by angels. In a workshop on the subject, people described being saved by an angel from drowning, from falling downstairs, from being hit by a truck.

Our churches, trapped since the Enlightenment in a posture that demands the provable, need to move and be stretched. It is time for the rigid categories and boundaries and classifications we have set up to be re-examined.

Things don't have to be either/or; they can be both/and.

A friend, Anne Squire, remembers being very sick in hospital after surgery. In an interview published in *The United Church Observer*, she recalled this incident:

I was having a very restless night with lots of pain, [when] suddenly I was absolutely sure that Christ was in the room with me – there was no doubt in my mind whatsoever – holding my hand.

The next night when the night nurse came in, she asked, "Are you going to be all right tonight?" And she explained, "You were in so much pain last night that I came and held your hand."

When I told that story afterwards, someone said, "Weren't you disappointed that it wasn't Christ, that it was just the nurse?"

*But it **was** Christ, and it **was** the nurse.*[7]

Given our computers' constant commands to be precise (ever tried responding "maybe" to a query from your PC?), it's tempting to allow yes/no thinking to become ingrained. But, away from the computer, yes/ no digital answers are not the only response humans can make. It is easy to be captured by the economics of a situation, for example. The numbers look so pure and beautiful. But we need to maintain our ability to be ambiguous, to mourn, to see the gray areas, and to draw wisdom from stories and legends as well as from numbers.

The sacred in the everyday

Reg Bibby, the sociologist, declares that Canadians love mystery. "Canadians not only believe in God in overwhelming numbers," he says. "Forty to 50 percent think they have experienced God. God is extremely popular, even if religion is not."[8]

If all those people have experienced God somehow, some way, and if so many are running into angels here and there – and that's not counting the ones who don't actually meet angels, but happily watch movies about them – the church needs to pay serious attention. Clearly, these are not all churchgoers. And that means they must be encountering God in some place other than at church.

Anyone who insists there is only one special time and place for worship and prayer, and only one special group of people who know the correct language and form, hasn't caught on to God's love of appearing in odd things like forests and cities and bluejays.

Congregations, therefore, need – like the Celts – to see heaven in a flaming maple. They need to allow themselves to be called "romantic" and "mystical." Congregations need to acknowledge and welcome people who feel righteous anger when a stream is destroyed and the salmon – the salmon that are in some mysterious way connected to them – can no longer rise.

Some church documents have struggled with this.

I'm proud of my denomination, The United Church of Canada, for including a line in its creed: "To live with respect in Creation."

The same denomination brought to its 36th General Council a document called *Mending the World* that asked us to see the world through eyes "blurred by tears" for the damage that has been done, and to look outward to the planet, not only inward to the church.

The world is in serious trouble, *Mending the World* says. Churches should join with people of goodwill, Christian or not, to work together for the cause of justice, peace, and the healing of God's creation. One writer expressed it this way in the report: "The chief ecumenical scandal of our time is not the disunity of the church. Rather it is the institutional preoccupation of the church in the face of the suffering of the world."[9]

Affirming a central principle

The document's emphatic placement of the care of the earth ahead of the church's own survival, and its reduced focus on Christianity's own multitude of denominations, raised some concerns at that Council. "You can choose your friends, but not your family," commented Sr. Donna Geernaert of the Canadian Conference of Catholic Bishops, for example. "We are the same family." Some also feared what they considered the document's "pluralistic theology."

But a willingness to die to self, if need be, in order to save the world is something for which there is good precedent in the Christian church. It's what Jesus did, and what we are called to do.

Mending the World goes on:

If we see ourselves only in a managerial relationship to nature, not much will change. Francis of Assisi had enough imagination to see himself related to other, non-human creatures as kin: Brother Sun and Sister Moon and Mother Earth. It was Francis who first set up a nativity manger scene. It was Francis who got the woolly lambs and cows and donkeys onto the stage of Christmas. Following his example, we might develop further our relationship to the earth as one of friendship.[10]

There are those who would argue that this is not a biblical perspective. The Bible deals a great deal with human relationships – with each other and with God. The Ten Commandments, these people would point out, say nothing about nature. Nor do Jesus' summations of the law.

Vanderbilt University theologian Sallie McFague has an answer to this view:

The Bible also does not say anything about freeing slaves. It doesn't say anything about the equal status of women.

We cannot expect the Bible to address all issues in all centuries. The question is, rather, is there a basic principle or paradigm at the center of Christian witness which can be applied to this issue? I think there is. It is the liberation understanding of Christianity, the radical destabilizing inclusive love of God for all – especially the oppressed and the outcast. This is how slaves and women got into the picture. Their cause didn't get in because it was named in scripture. The only group named there is the poor, the oppressed, the outcasts. Other groups have gotten in because they fit under that principle. I think the natural world does too.

Modern technological development has given us the ability to do enormous destruction to the natural world. We humans have so much power that nature has to be seen as one of "the poor." Nature is oppressed, and we are the oppressors.[11]

What if...?

We cannot turn the clock back. But perhaps we could make it less difficult to be at peace with the universe.

- What if our Christian Education centers offered special weeks for contemplatives, simple small huts in the woods for silence and prayer? We all need times to talk about serious subjects; but when a whole continent longs for God (and Bibby's data says it does) we could use a chance to see God's face in quiet as well.

- What if denominations treasured their church camps and retreat centers as their most valuable properties, their chances to be in touch with Creation?

- What if, in the summer, worship was sometimes out-of-doors? What if it didn't always consist of a sermon and some hymns – what if sometimes it was a pilgrimage to the woods (if there are any) or fields or streets?

- What if there were gardens around every church building, growing vegetables for the food bank and flowers for the Communion table? Sacrament and social justice together, a lovely symbol of balance in our congregational life. Beauty and truth. Bread and roses.
- What if our new mission fields were, literally, to the fields? What if congregations and denominational structures together supported volunteers or paid workers in the way of the old mission societies? Only this time, they would support those who could give up their work for a time to care for the land through political advocacy or physical labor.
- What if congregations routinely sponsored intergenerational cleanups, because we knew that caring for the earth was itself a form of worship?
- What if seminaries, in offering contextual theology, invited elderly farmers and birdwatchers to talk about the changes they have seen in Creation: birds that have had to move to new habitat, fields depleted by overintensive farming, weather patterns that have shifted?
- What if – even more radically – we taught ourselves in our congregations how to lie down in front of bulldozers, and how to remain calm when being baited and vilified?
- What if – as Ruether suggests – congregations became "base communities of spirituality and support"? Sometimes our hymns, preaching, Bible study, worship, and outreach might all voice our pain at the disease of our Mother Earth, instead of trying to pretend she doesn't exist. Other times, care for Creation might simply celebrate its beauty and diversity.

All this may seem idealistic. But we are already idealistic in congregations. That's why we have them. We make them a place where everyone gathers. Including those who don't normally associate with differing perspectives. An industrialist and an environmentalist might sit side by side on Sunday morning. The future church would continue to encourage them to talk to one another in peace and love. People can listen carefully to all sides of an argument and support whatever position is caring for the earth.

And wouldn't, then, the children come back to church?

Hope for the best

Perhaps my son was wrong; human rights *do* matter. Humans are one of God's creatures, and they deserve to be cared for.

But he was also right. The fabric of life is all of a piece. The energy that stamps casually on a bug or swerves a car to run over a slow-moving porcupine is evidence of Paul's "principalities and powers" at work, just as much as when those powers throw a dissenter in China into prison, initiate "ethnic cleansing" in the Balkans, or launch a covert assault on democracy in Central America. We need to mourn for, cherish, and celebrate in hymns the land that owns us.

The church has to underpin this with a theology for our time. We don't have it yet – but we are working at it, in bits and pieces, here and there.

Most of all, we need our congregations to be filled with hope for Creation's restoration. When Jonah finally got to Nineveh, and preached as God had commanded, the Ninevites turned around and did as God asked. It must have been amazing, just as if everyone in North America suddenly refused to drive cars whose emissions hurt the atmosphere; or insisted on having solar panels for the roofs of their houses, or made gardens for the pleasure of others.

Our congregations need to believe, always, that good is about to happen. Like the scoundrel Jacob going to meet the brother whose blessing he had stolen, we need to understand we will be embraced even if we have sinned. Even if we are still learning to be compassionate towards the earth.

The Whole Person

CHRISTOPHER WHITE

*When the man saw that he did not prevail against Jacob, he
struck him on the hip socket; and Jacob's hip was put out of
joint as he wrestled with him…The sun rose upon him as he
passed Penuel, limping because of his hip.*
Genesis 32:25, 31

Just 24 hours after she was born, our youngest daughter Elizabeth had heart
surgery. At ten months of age, she had an open heart correction and a kid-
ney repair. And two years ago to the day, as I write this chapter, she entered
Toronto's Hospital for Sick Children for her fourth operation, her second
open-heart surgery.

I recall our feelings well. We were a mess. My wife Wendy and I were
frightened. Because of the risk, of course. But also because of a flood of
unhappy memories from the last time when things did not, at first, go well.
Our eldest daughter Sarah, old enough to remember visiting baby Elizabeth
in an Intensive Care Unit in Edmonton, was grieving deeply. Her normally
bubbling joy had disappeared.

Elizabeth herself, at age five, was resigned to her operation. She was
probably stronger than any of us. She walked down to the operating room

with the nurse, still wearing her snow boots, convinced that later that day she would walk back out of there.

We settled in for a six- to eight-hour wait in the surgical waiting room. My best friend Bob was already waiting for us there with cards, a cribbage board, and a pile of magazines. We played cards and waited. And waited…

While Elizabeth was undergoing her surgery, the worst blizzard of the year hit the Toronto area. In the middle of it all, something quite wonderful happened, what I call a wonder of faith.

All through the day people trooped into my church, Westminster United. They were members of the church, and they were from throughout the community. In spite of the blizzard, they came to pray, to wait with us in spirit, and to lift up Elizabeth to God. All day and into the evening they came, in ones and twos, the church never empty, a candle in the shape of a dove burning on the Communion table. The night before, they had gathered for a special service of prayer for her.

To be supported in prayer that way was amazing. We were never alone. Prayers were always with us.

Six hours after Elizabeth went into the operating theatre her surgeon came out. The surgery had gone exceptionally well. He had performed a new procedure that promised a much longer period before her next operation would be required. We could go into the intensive care unit to see her. Elizabeth was a mass of tubes. But as she woke up, she literally tried to get up off the bed and go home. They had to restrain her or she would have made it.

A week later, in one of the most amazing recoveries I have seen, Elizabeth was home.

A little over a month ago, as I write this, she had her annual checkup at the Hospital for Sick Children. Her cardiologist said it was a "superb surgical outcome." She's strong, healthy, and full of energy. We still worry whenever she looks tired, or runs a temperature. But she is (touch wood!) great.

Confused about healing

Do I attribute her amazing recovery simply to the power of prayer? No, I do not. She had one of the best cardiac surgeons, in one the best children's hospitals, combined with her own amazing internal strength and determination. But I do believe that her recovery was enhanced by the prayers of our community. And I know that her parents and sister would not have come through the experience as well as we did without our parish nurse who walked with us through this ordeal and organized the prayers and services on Elizabeth's behalf.

We in the mainstream churches are skittish about healing in the church. The very concept evokes images of Elmer Gantry, of crooked faith healers out to fleece the gullible flocks. We are skeptical, suspicious, and sometimes scornful of anything that sounds like a healing ministry.

I don't know why we have this attitude. Jesus came to preach, to teach, and to heal. His healing got him in as much trouble with the authorities as anything else that he said or did. John's gospel portrays the raising of Lazarus, not the overturning of the moneychangers in the Temple, as the last straw for the authorities, the political act that leads to Jesus' crucifixion.

As Tom Harpur pointed out in his book *The Uncommon Touch*, healing has been a central act and focus of the Christian Church from the very beginning. Similarly, Rochelle Graham writes, in *Healing from the Heart*, "Part of the faith of the early Christians was that their God was a loving, compassionate, healing God who expected a healing ministry from Christian followers."[1]

Graham, a practitioner of Healing Touch, continues:

I find a great deal of confusion – to my surprise, especially among church people – about healing.

We need to make a distinction between "healing" and "curing." It's possible to be cured without being healed, and it's equally possible to be healed without being cured. The medical professions, generally, concentrate on cures; it has cynically been said that, in fact, all they seek to cure are the symptoms. If you have blurred sight, an ophthalmologist can restore clear vision with prescription eyeglasses, and you're considered cured. Healing, however, seeks to repair and restore everything that surrounds the symptom...

Consider a hard-driving, hard-drinking, hard-headed business executive. His lifestyle leads to a heart attack. Bypass surgery – or a heart transplant – cures the specific problem. He now has a perfectly sound heart again. But does he have a sound lifestyle? Sound relationships with his staff, his customers? Does he live in better harmony with the world around him?

In such a case, healing would look very different from curing.[2]

Her distinction might be even more obvious, if we remember the story of Jacob. After his struggle with the angel, by the banks of the Jabbok River, Jacob did not have a wounded hip cured. Indeed, just the opposite – he walked with a limp for the rest of his life. But he did experience healing. Instead of constantly fleeing from his actions, he was able to go forward confidently to reconciliation with his brother; he matured into the revered patriarch of what would eventually become the twelve tribes of the nation of Israel.

Just as the people in first century Palestine needed the healing offered by Jesus, and after him by his disciples, so do we in our stressed out, frantic paced, 21st century world. We too are a frightened, angry people, overwhelmed by events beyond our control. Caught in a crack of history, still absorbing the full consequences of the computer and the global economy, we are reeling. We need healing.

A constant concern

In Canada, health care has become a national concern, almost a hallmark of Canadian identity. Almost daily, we are reminded that our healthcare system is in crisis. Waiting lists for anything from cancer treatment to cardiac surgery remain an ongoing threat to individual survival. As I write, 14 emergency rooms in Toronto were turning away patients yesterday – there was no room for more patients.

Meanwhile, our federal and provincial governments continue to assure us that up is down, that red is green, and that everything in health care is working. Yet it is their policies that have starved the medical system of proper funding and led us to potential calamity. Increasingly, I believe they have a silent agenda, to introduce two-tiered medicine in Canada. Provincial governments in Ontario and Alberta have taken the lead. With their obvious distaste for all public institutions, they have systematically attacked public servants, from their own employees to nurses and teachers. Public is bad, private is good.

David Frum, the *enfant terrible* of the new right, writes a column in the *National Post,* Canada's newspaper of the right. Before the last provincial election, Frum wrote that the Ontario Conservatives need to convince the public "that the old system is unworkable" so that a free market reform of health care can take its place. In Alberta, only sanctions by the federal government prevented a limited two-tier system from being introduced.

One argument made by proponents of privatized medicine is that this will reduce pressure on the public system, making more resources available for those who need it.

The British experience demonstrates the falsity of this reasoning. Britain offers two healthcare systems: the publicly funded universal National Health Service, and a private health insurance system. The result has not been a "freeing" of resources for the NHS; instead, long waits plague the public system. The London newspaper, *The Evening Standard*, recently reported the deaths of two men from heart failure. Both were on long waiting lists for cardiac surgery.[3] One was a cab driver, the other a grocer. Had they the financial means, they could have paid for private care and received the operations they needed. In Britain today, wealth gets you to the front of the line; everyone else must wait, and sometimes die while doing so.

This is a cautionary tale for Canadians and those who think that two-tiered medicine can alleviate our problems.

In spite of the current difficulties being experienced by our system, Canadians have consistently shown that they want to preserve medicare. The additional funds promised by the federal government to the provinces are one sign that our politicians may be getting the message.

But make no mistake, the health system that Canadians have come to take for granted is under attack.

For Americans, the challenges are quite different. Health care there is already largely turned over to market forces. Insurance rates make affordable health care more and more difficult to obtain; the number of those with no health insurance or inadequate coverage grows daily. Health care becomes increasingly the prerogative of those who can afford it.

A new role for our churches

In this context, anything that churches can do to promote health and healing is bound to have an immediate and powerful impact on the community. I say that from personal experience.

There are, of course, many ways that churches can get involved in healing ministries. And I am definitely not advocating that I, or any other minister, should suddenly decide to hold healing sessions at the chancel steps which attempt to convert dental cavities into gold fillings by faith alone! But there is an enormous range of possibilities. A number of churches in western Canada have incorporated Healing Touch, Therapeutic Touch, or Reiki sessions into their ministry. Others promote a greater harmony of body, mind, and spirit by sponsoring Tai Chi or yoga groups. The Lowville Prayer Centre, now based at the Five Oaks lay training center near Paris, Ontario, has provided leadership in developing prayer groups and healing liturgies within the traditional context of Christian worship. I can't possibly describe all the options in a single chapter – it took Flora Litt, Wayne Irwin, and Rochelle Graham a whole book even to sample those possibilities! If you want to know more, I recommend their book, *Healing from the Heart: A Guide to Christian Healing for Individuals and Groups,* published by Wood Lake Books in 1998.

My experience is with a single small component of that whole range of healing ministries – the concept of having a parish nurse. But having seen what that program has done for our local congregation and community, I can affirm both the value of healing ministry for the church, and the hunger for it among church people.

But, some would argue, isn't the church feeding into the two-tier model of health care if it provides what amounts to private health care for its own members with a parish nurse?

Not at all. There is an enormous difference between a service restricted to those with the means to pay, and a ministry offered to a community of faith and to those beyond our walls, regardless of income. We need to combine our spirituality and our physicality. And we need help in negotiating the ever-fraying maze of government health services.

In case you missed the reference near the beginning of this chapter, it was our parish nurse who organized the prayer services at the time of my daughter Elizabeth's open-heart surgery.

Carolyn and Brian have three children. One of them, a boy named Adam, has both developmental and social challenges. Adam's parents were concerned that he was becoming isolated; he needed to experience life with other people. Our parish nurse made it known that we needed some families to help out. Westminster now has a network of five families helping Carolyn and Brian. Each week, Adam goes to spend part of the weekend with one of these families. The arrangement has benefited all parties immeasurably. Adam develops his social skills, his parents receive respite care, and the five families who have welcomed a new person into their lives learn to see their world in a different light.

The health ministry of our parish nurse has added a depth to our church and to my ministry that didn't exist before. We have held blood pressure clinics, run workshops on everything from stress management to a simplified Christmas to organic gardening. We've run a health fair, which included a chiropractor, a Therapeutic Touch practitioner, and a reflexologist. We just completed a wonderful marriage enrichment day attended by 15 couples. Nor is this growth of interest limited to physical or material concerns. A small group that we call a "Health Cabinet" – composed of congregation members, the nurse, and myself – have organized Advent services, special Lenten study series, and the Maundy Thursday service.

All of these programs have linked together our spiritual and physical health.

How a program grows

The concept of a parish nurse originated in Germany with the Lutheran church. In the 19th century, congregations had "community sisters" who looked after the health needs of their members. But when those Lutherans emigrated to the United States and Canada, the community sister concept did not make the trip over the Atlantic with them.

In 1978, Granger Westburg, at that time the chaplain at Lutheran General Hospital in Chicago, wrote a little book called *Good Grief.* He was concerned that the medical model of health care was completely divorced from spirituality. He wanted to create a Holistic Health Center at the hospital staffed by a doctor, a nurse, and a psychologist. He hoped that bringing these three together would allow healing of the whole person, rather than merely curing a symptom.

For a variety of reasons, his holistic model failed. But out of it came the parish nurse idea. Westburg noticed that the nurse was the one who consistently attended to the patient's spiritual needs. As a result, ten years later, in 1988, Lutheran General funded a pilot project placing six nurses in congregations of different denominational backgrounds. It was a huge success. The idea spread throughout the United States.

The concept came to Canada in the summer of 1993 when a Lutheran pastor, the Rev. Henry Fischer, was visiting his brother in Bethlehem, Pennsylvania. While there he started to feel quite ill. The church's parish nurse took his blood pressure. She discovered that he was at risk and urged him to see a doctor as soon as he returned to Ontario.

Two days after he got home, his phone rang. It was the parish nurse from Pennsylvania, calling to make sure that he had gone to the doctor. He hadn't, but her caring prompted him to make an appointment at once. He learned that he required immediate medication for his blood pressure. Without that nurse's intervention, he could have been heading toward a stroke.

Henry was so impressed by the effectiveness of that nurse that he began to wonder if the parish nurse concept would work in Canada. Whether by coincidence or divine intervention, shortly after that he received a phone call from Audrey Fisher, a United Church minister and nurse, and Maureen

Macleod, who had her own nursing practice, to talk about the possibility of creating parish nursing in Canada. By the spring of 1994, Inter Church Health Ministries had been set up, with five pilot projects in the region east of Toronto.

As in the U.S., all were a huge success. Now there are 38 congregations and agencies with a parish nurse, with more on the way all over Ontario.

Henry Fischer was named Executive Director of Inter Church Health Ministries in 1996. "I've never had so much fun in my life," he exults. Parish nursing, he told me, is spreading "like a prairie wildfire across Canada." Every mainline denomination is getting onboard.

An antidote to depression

More than just providing nursing care, this example of healing ministry is creating hope and excitement in congregations.

Henry Fischer has worked in all sorts of churches recently. Like me, he's concerned about aging and declining membership, simmering anger at pastoral leadership, limited financial resources, and churches showing signs of what he labels as "clinical depression." The parish nursing movement has created a sense of mission in these declining congregations. It has played an intrinsic role in revitalization. The churches themselves receive healing, and pass it on to others.

To be successful, parish nursing must, in Fischer's view, be "theologically based, congregationally driven, and mission and ministry focused." This is a genuine grassroots movement being driven by the people in the pews. In many cases, national denominational leadership is still too preoccupied with funding shortfalls and program cutbacks to grasp its implications for the wider church.

Fortunately, there has been some institutional support. In my area, Oshawa Presbytery of the United Church of Canada has funded this project since its inception. Their support gave Inter Church Health Ministries the financial means to set up an office, pay staff, and initiate their education program for congregations. Now other denominations are considering partnership with

ICHM. Emmanuel College, part of the Toronto School of Theology, is also playing an important part, offering a diploma program in Health Ministry.

Changing people and communities

A health ministry can not only change a congregation – it changes people, too. Westminster United Church's parish nurse is Gail Brimbecom. She still remembers exactly where she was standing when the phone rang and Joan Sanderson (a parish nursing pioneer) asked her to serve on the first ICHM board. It was for Gail the ultimate epiphany experience. In a flash, she knew what she had been meant to do with her life.

As our parish nurse, she finally has the opportunity to deal with all aspects of the person for whom she is caring. "This work is a gift," she told me recently. "It's a humbling experience walking with people in this role."

Gail Brimbecom sees the ministry she does as a way of multiplying the ministers within the congregation. Irene Gow, for example, attended a parish nursing presentation one Sunday. After the presentation, Irene looked around and was suddenly aware of the number of widows in the church. She decided to begin a monthly "Women living alone" lunch. Women heard about the idea and started calling her even before she could get in touch with them. What she had expected to be a group of seven or so grew to close to 30. Now, regularly, they have an opportunity to share food and common concerns: everything from health and family to the challenges of living alone. A new community was born, a new ministry launched.

For her part, Gail is determined to extend her ministry into the wider community. Her concerns are both health care and health issues. She feels that the church is one of the few institutions left that can speak with integrity against the agenda of continuing privatization.

Parish nursing enabled Westminster to grow. In its sense of community, and in its sense of service. To renew our congregations we need to rediscover our health ministry. By becoming a healing community we rediscover what brought the church together in the first place.

Together in faith

And my Elizabeth? We go for bike rides together. She will appear in a featured role as a horse in her upcoming ballet recital. And she can do a mean "hot pepper" as she skips rope.

Do I still worry? Of course I do. I'm her dad, and I'll always worry. But she is a gift from God. She is doing wonderfully, and so am I. For I am now more convinced than ever that her health and well-being is not something separate from my Christian faith as an individual and my professional work as a minister, but is integral to it.

Partners in Spirituality

DONNA SINCLAIR

Then the man said, "You shall no longer be called Jacob,
but Israel, for you have striven with God and with humans,
and have prevailed."
Genesis 32:28

A new heart I will give you, and a new spirit I will put within
you; and I will remove from your body the heart of stone and
give you a heart of flesh. I will put my spirit within you, and
make you follow my ordinances.
Then you shall live in the land I gave your ancestors;
and you shall be my people.
Ezekiel 36:26–28

We were gathered in a loose circle in the church gymnasium. It was evening, dark; the only light came from a scattering of candles around the huge room. Inside the circle was a large drum with four chairs pulled up to it. Throughout the evening, various people – whoever wished, adults and children – took turns pounding a steady rhythm set by Terry Dokis, the Ojibway elder who had brought the drum.

He had also set up an enormous labyrinth, patterned after the one found in the great cathedral in Chartres, France. It consumed much of the rest of the gym floor.

The room was heavy with the scent of pine from branches surrounding this ancient design. There were carefully composed symbols at the east, south, west, and north of it. Water, fire, earth, and air each had a place at one of the four directions. And people were walking the labyrinth, accompanied by the calming, comforting, steadying heartbeat of the drum.

Dokis has been leading a revival of interest in this symbol in our city. The labyrinth is a pre-Christian design that was enthusiastically adopted by Christians in the Middle Ages, making its way into their cathedrals. With its slow, circuitous pathway inward and outward, it fed the mystical spirit of the age. And its intricate length provided a path, in a pilgrimage-conscious age, for those who wanted to live out their faith with their bodies by walking and praying, but couldn't go to the Holy Land.

Dokis sees a strong similarity to the medicine wheel of Native spirituality.

Its presence at our annual congregational retreat made it much more than a time of reflection. The evening became a symbol of the blessings that continue to be offered to the Christian church from the First Nations.

From them, I believe, our churches could receive a new heart – one that beats to a rhythm and is animated by a spirit springing from this side of the Atlantic.

The marks of this spirit are simple but radical: love for the land that is respectful and conscious of its sacredness. A way of meeting together that listens patiently and aims for consensus. Above all, a powerful spirituality filled with gratitude and a sense of mystery.

That, says Reginald Bibby (having polled the nation), is something Canadians long for. He explains this using a market analogy (which upsets many in the churches) to make the point clear:

Everyone's research, including mine, comes up with a consistent finding: over the years, a rich market for supernatural and spiritual matters has persisted… The news is not that God is alive. God has always been alive. The news is that interest and intrigue persist, in spite of the problems of organized religion. The result may well be a very sizable, ongoing spiritual vacuum because…the key religious firms are failing.[1]

Peoples who have retained their spirituality in the face of determined efforts to stamp it out surely have something precious to teach the Christian church. University of Calgary professor John Friesen describes the powerful sense that the Stoney people, for example, have of "a world designed, created, and managed by God, The Creator or Sky Father… The spirit of an animal was entreated and thanked before the creature was taken for food. The plant spirit was contacted when a plant was utilized for medicinal or spiritual purposes."[2]

Friesen describes this constant interaction between the spirit and the material world (quite similar, to my mind, to the constant interaction between the Celts and a host of angels) and continues:

Had the Europeans made note of this at the time of the time of the first contact they might not have found it quite as necessary to engage so fervently in making disciples. Rather they might have more profitably spent their time comparing notes and expanding their own spiritual vocabulary and perspective.[3]

It's not too late to do that expansion.

Closed minds, closed hearts

I write as a Canadian Christian. The story of our relationship with the First Nations of the northern half of this continent is a long one, and it differs often from the story south of us.

One place to pick that story up would be in 1986, on a gravel parking lot in Sudbury, Ont., where the United Church of Canada apologized to Native congregations, because "in our zeal to tell you the good news of Jesus Christ, we were closed to the value of your spirituality."[4]

Later, in 1993, the primate of the Anglican Church of Canada offered a similar formal apology for "the church's failure" in the residential schools, acknowledging to the people at a national Native convocation that "we failed you. We failed ourselves. We failed God."[5]

Both of these were long overdue statements. The Canadian churches and the federal government had been integral to an enterprise aimed at assimilating Native people and making them essentially non-Native. The effort included government regulation against ceremonies and dances all over the country, silencing the sacred songs, outlawing the potlatch. As Doreen Clellamin of Bella Coola, BC, said during meetings before that apology, "People on some reserves tell me that all their songs are borrowed, all the dances are borrowed. Their own are gone from the reserve forever, locked in their elders' lives."[6]

There was no more sustained assault on Native spirituality than the effort to make Native children into white people by enrolling them forcibly into residential schools.

The impetus for residential schools was an odd mixture of altruism, arrogance, and condescension. Some Native people recognized that the world was changing, and actually requested schools. But the kind of schools they got was fueled by an understanding on the part of non-Native Canadians that, in hindsight, can only be labeled racist: the assumption that with enough time, education, and discipline, Native people would become just like white people. Beginning (roughly) in the mid-19th century, the four mainline Canadian churches – Roman Catholic, Anglican, Methodist (later United), and Presbyterian – ran the schools for almost a hundred years, convinced that the students (and their parents) were in need of salvation from their heritage by the Christian message.

The federal government – aware of the twin advantages of low-cost employees supplied by the churches, and a new system of imposed beliefs congruent with Canadian society – happily funded these schools. As one government report declared:

It must be obvious that to teach semi-civilized children is a more difficult task than to teach children with inherited aptitudes, whose training is, moreover, carried on at home… The advantage of calling in the aid of religion is, that there is a chance of getting an enthusiastic person with…a motive power beyond anything pecuniary remuneration could supply. The work requires not only the energy but the patience of an enthusiast. [7]

For three generations, children were taken from their parents at a young age and kept away from what was regarded as the regressive tendencies of their own homes. With treatment that ranged from genuine affection to ferocity, often forbidden to speak their language, they were inculcated with as much of white culture as could be squeezed into them.

Because they were alone and vulnerable, and because their complaints were often ignored, some children were sexually abused. At the time of writing, there are 1400 civil lawsuits against the churches in question and the federal government. In most cases, the plaintiffs describe sexual and/or physical abuse, although a few cases are being brought to the courts on the grounds of destruction of culture.

But for 500 years, battered and eroded and driven underground, those Native cultures had survived. Despite residential schools, arbitrary regulations that placed Native farmers at a disadvantage in some areas, the steady pressure on land for oil and gas extraction or mining or highways or hydroelectric development, the deterioration of waters that many fished, and above all the stereotyping of their people, somehow the gifts of Native spirituality remained.

And Terry Dokis, traditional Ojibway, now brought a drum, the heartbeat of Mother Earth, into a Christian church in an extraordinary act of forgiveness and hope. By restoring the labyrinth to us, he was restoring our own Good News.

Transforming hearts of stone

Native people didn't come through unscathed, of course. Courtrooms are the setting now for dreadful stories of brokenness and loss of identity, played out for some in alcoholism, abuse, and suicide.

But the core of a battered peoples' relationship to the Creator is still there. It's alive and very powerful in – for instance – the writing of Thomas King or Richard Wagamese; the paintings of Leland Bell, *Bebaminojmat;* the carvings of Bill Reid. And it is especially available to the churches in those Native members who, often at great cost, lean like human bridges across cultures, interpreting, explaining.

Slowly, they transform our hearts of stone. The Very Rev. Stan McKay, for example, is Cree, and a United Church minister. When he served as moderator, our church's highest elected office, he respectfully held up the traditional values of his people, bringing those values to his church: the inseparability of spirituality from education; the priority given to family; the value of consensus.

An understanding of the possibility contained in narrative was part of that. Once I listened spellbound while he told an audience of mainly non-Native people the story of a guest who comes to a house and gradually takes over the whole place, room by room, refusing to leave and finally relegating the original occupants to the basement. I believe it was, for some listeners, the first they had understood the impact of their own ancestors' arrival in this land.

Native people within the churches are giving us an enlarged understanding of certain concepts we thought we already knew. As the world evolves into a global village, the gap between rich and poor, both nations and people, threatens to turn into an uncrossable abyss. We need the tribal values that we could learn from Native peoples. As nation-states crumble into ineffective fragments where politicians have ceded power to the chief executive officers of multinational corporations, these values may yet save us.

Forgiveness

"I'm sorry," for example. "I apologize."

In my United Church, after the launch of a civil suit to obtain compensation for victims of sexual abuse at the Port Alberni residential school, those words seemed at first to stick in our collective throat. Church members feared that by speaking them, the denomination would nullify its insurance coverage and be liable for millions of dollars.

It led to a peculiar situation. The national media – watching the church try to call the federal government to account for its share of the wrongs – rightly accused it of squandering its moral capital in an attempt to save its economic life. At the same time, many Native people made it clear they didn't want an apology that was simply words. They were, in fact, waiting to see how the "I'm sorry" from 1986 would be lived out.

But one day in 1998, after a long meeting of church representatives, a long Bible study, a long look at the gospel, and a hearing of some of the stories from the schools, they managed to say the words. And the Christian term "repentance" took on marvelous shades of meaning. The current moderator, the Right Rev. Bill Phipps, said,

I am here today as Moderator of The United Church of Canada to speak the words that many people have wanted to hear for a very long time. On behalf of The United Church of Canada I apologize for the pain and suffering that our church's involvement in the Indian Residential School system has caused. We are aware of some of the damage that this cruel and ill-conceived system of assimilation has perpetrated on Canada's First Nations peoples. For this we are truly and most humbly sorry.[8]

The members of the denominational executive that made that decision understood it would not be possible to bring everyone in the church on board before the step was taken. Some would have to learn nuances of the word repentance, and their own history, as they went.

We know that many within our church will still not understand why each of us must bear the scar, the blame for this horrendous period in Canadian history. But the truth is we are the bearers of many blessings from our ancestors, and therefore we must also bear their burdens. We must now seek ways of healing ourselves, as well as our relationships with First Nations peoples. This apology is not an end in itself. We are in the midst of a long and painful journey.[9]

Humility

The first real public test of the United Church's 1986 apology had come in August, 1990, long before Phipps made the statement above. The United Church was meeting as a General Council in southwestern Ontario. Five hundred miles away, the width of the province away, a road had been barricaded by Mohawk people at Kanesatake (Oka), Quebec. In solidarity with them, a bridge had been blocked at Kahnawake, not far away – the extremely busy link between the city of Montreal and one of its suburbs. The Canadian army had been called in. The entire country, glued in shock to television screens, watched Canadian armored personnel carriers grinding through Canadian streets.

Meantime, at the General Council, a gray-haired Cree woman went quietly to the microphone. "We call ourselves believers in the Creator," said Evelyn Broadfoot, "and yet we cannot support our people that are struggling, our children and our grandmothers that are crying." Broadfoot looked around at the other commissioners, her voice full of authority. "We need you to stand beside us, just like what we said when you apologized to us."

And they did. It was clear, as the delegates listened, that the arrogance behind what one early missionary tract referred to as the "great plains waiting to be harvested" – the original concept of mission in this country – had changed. The church's outgoing moderator, the Very Rev. Sang Chul Lee, a tiny Korean with a long wispy white beard, had already spent time in Kanesatake, standing with the Mohawk people under siege.

It is possible this marks a difference between Canadian and American churches. We have not had to deal with a history of black slavery. But we have been forced to acknowledge, and to try to redeem, our triumphalist history with Native people. In court, around meeting tables, in lunch rooms and church halls, climbing on to buses with protesters going to jail. We have learned what it means to have been wrong, and to have done wrong.

Not all of us, in the mainline churches here. We have not all come to that realization yet. But by their presence and their bitter, hard-told stories,

Native Christians have touched other delegates at church meetings. Sometimes they have made them cry. And every time that happens, a heart of stone breaks and becomes a holy place.

We are a healthier Christian church as a result of this long conversation between Native and non-Native members. The consequence of saying "I'm sorry," could be financial upheaval for a huge institution. But receiving a new heart is never cheap or easy.

The Bible tells us that Jacob, too, paid a high price for his change of heart. He spent the rest of his life limping. But in exchange, he gained a brother, and founded a tribe.

People matter

Time is less important than people. I remember a baptism in the little Anglican church near Schefferville, Quebec, attended by a people in those days referred to by outsiders as the Naskapi, and who are now known by their own name, the Innu. When the ceremony was over, every person present, in turn, came and kissed the baby, welcoming the child to their midst.

It took longer than any other baptismal service I have witnessed.

At every First Nations ceremony I have ever attended, there is a similar slow, patient, attentiveness to every person present. Even reporters (this is always startling to me) are invited into the circle, perhaps offered the honor of saying a prayer. It is assumed that all people are worthy.

The group takes precedence

In First Nations' traditions, the tribe is more important than the individual. That principle goes against the grain of our contemporary culture, which has made individual rights one step short of sacred.

It used to be our principle, too. Sociologist Reginald Bibby argues in *Mosaic Madness* that "from the time our ancestors took their first teetering steps on the planet, they recognized that it was easier to stay alive and live well if they stuck together."[10]

Unfortunately, that recognition is under attack. More and more, people prefer to isolate themselves than to stick together. Gated communities spring up. Welfare support is slashed, increasing the number of impoverished children. Disabled people, and those who care for them, reel as funding for special needs vanishes. Construction of low-cost housing stops, and homelessness increases. Says Bibby bleakly:

The need for balance between the individual and the group urgently needs to be reaffirmed. Rampant individualism will obliterate social life. It will make interaction empty and relationships tenuous, family life unstable and the workplace less productive, education custom-made and religion a consumer item, citizenship and community involvement nothing but means to self-serving ends. [11]

That's not the way it works with First Nations people. Not even after 500 years of being battered as communities. Witness Ojibway novelist Richard Wagamese, writing in *A Quality of Light*. "We are all tribal people," he says. Tribalism lies within each of us as

A vague stirring of desire to be included in the warmth, the security, of a community, a circle easing together around a common fire, safe from the encroaching darkness. Perhaps we need to remind each other we have these old fires in common… That each of us, in the great story that is the history of our people, carries the memory of the one, nurtured, protected and enhanced by the whole… That we are human beings and the night is always around us.[12]

When a congregation reaches out to the people around it, trying to bring wholeness in the form of economic justice for the needy, or spiritual renewal for the weary, we act out of that same great memory. Jesus gave us the stories to sustain that memory. And Jacob, of course, was familiar with the "night around us." That's where he met God.

Respectful relationships

"Respect" is a word with a far larger meaning than the dominant culture usually gives it. Respect is shown to the elders (who are not necessarily elderly) for their wisdom; to the small creatures of the earth, the worms and beetles, for the essential work they do in keeping the soil alive; to other humans by listening carefully to their words.

When that notion of respect is adopted as an expression of faith, it might help save the earth – to say nothing of our relationships with each other, and with God.

One possible interpretation of Jacob's struggle with the angel in the night is that he didn't want to listen. He had no respect for others; he did what he wanted. And he didn't want to hear what God had to say to him about his self-centered and individualistic attitude. That unwillingness, that resistance, was rendered metaphorically by the biblical storytellers as a physical struggle.

Spirituality

The spiritual leader is recognized by the people to have special abilities; he or she understands that personal pride and privilege have no part in the status given him or her by others.

The ability to travel into the heart of God's mystery – what we would call mysticism – is the gift of the shaman. Shamans are not limited to Native tradition. Jacob was probably a shaman; Jesus certainly was. But if our churches are to rediscover the role of the shaman in spiritual growth, we may have to learn it from our Native brothers and sisters.

The fabled "seekers," the ones who yearn for spirituality but don't know where to look, may understand the crucial role of shamans in religious faith without naming them as such. Pointing out the quantities of "paranormal" experiences reported by Canadians, sociologist Bibby observes that it is "peculiar" that these experiences are ignored by academics. "As for God," he says, "close to one in two think they have experienced God's presence."[13]

And he goes on:

What's peculiar is the extent to which these commonplace experiences have been slow to receive official recognition. Surveys and late-night conversations reveal that…they are the norm rather than the exception. Yet [these] events have been largely ignored…by close-minded academics who, frankly, have done us all a serious disservice… As Gary Wills puts it, "The learned have their own superstitions, prominent among them a belief that superstition is evaporating."[14]

We need to encourage congregational leaders and spiritual directors who have the strength to enter into mystery. We need people who can recognize, listen, and help interpret those moments when God seems very near – alone, or in communal worship, or in Bible study, or in groups that meet specifically to help spirituality mature through dreams or prayer or conversation.

We needn't fear this, as long as denominations train their professional clergy well. Part of the wisdom of the institutional church has always been its ability to place safeguards around such experiences. Tools for discernment – so that participants can discover if this is truly God they are conversing with – are as crucial as knowledge of church history or skill in chairing a meeting.

The treasure of tradition

We need to take care of our legends. North American culture faces a crisis of meaning partly because it is losing the stories that give life its shape – particularly the biblical narratives and poems and appeals that have helped generations of people make sense out of their life experiences. As more and more people spend their time at the mall or the arena on Sunday morning instead of in church, the collective memory of an entire people erodes. The stories of Jacob and Jesus, of Rachel and Mary – or, for that matter, of Mohammed or Buddha – are replaced by commercial slogans for McDonald's and Nike.

But we could learn to regard our stories with a fuller awareness of the treasures they contain. As Friesen points out, most tribes valued and carefully safeguarded their origin legends: "Selected individuals would learn the story by careful listening; then, on mastering the story, would pass it on."[15] Along with other aspects of their spirituality, these legends "represented spiritual connections between people and the universe which, with appropriate care, resulted in a lifestyle of assured food supply, physical well-being, and the satisfying of the needs and wants of the society and its members."[16]

Our scriptures also began as oral tales. They give us a buffer against many aspects of culture from which – as people who espouse compassion and the common good – we feel increasingly exiled. At the same time, they help us make sense out of what is happening to us, and give us hope. Our ancestors also lived in strange lands where they were not at home – Egypt and Babylon – and they learned and survived and returned. We can too.

The care of the biblical narrative, the teaching of its truths to our people, is a task the church must undertake with a sense of its enormous urgency. We can learn how from those First Nations who, against terrible odds, kept their stories alive for five hundred years, locked in dances and songs– just as our own stories are often locked in liturgy and hymns.

Accessible wisdom

If you have read this far, you may be ready to declare this whole chapter an exercise in romanticism, the wishful thinking of a white woman who wants to be Native. A woman cheerfully ready to give up her own Christian convictions as if they didn't matter.

Not so. The problem is not the difficult and priceless commands of Jesus, not the marvel of the incarnation, the mystery of the Trinity, the stories. These form the structure of my much-loved house of faith.

But no-one ever said a house couldn't change with the years. No one would ever suggest it wouldn't need a new roof, or an addition as the family grew. And faith is as organic as every other human enterprise.

If we had allowed the concept of the earth-as-holy to enter our faith, if we had been open to the idea of a land full of spirit, perhaps we would not wage the kind of war on the land that may someday destroy it.

For instance, as I write, news reports describe the sell-off of pure water from Ontario's aquifers – 18 billion litres a year – despite concerns that it cannot be replaced. We have always refused to sell blood in Canada; we accept it only from volunteers, and take only what they can replace with health. But – in this case – we have little compunction about selling the lifeblood of the earth.

All this may sound as if I do not honor the gifts of passion and love that missionaries often brought to those they served. I do. I also believe that advancement in the ability to extract water from deep wells, say, marks a society becoming more technologically advanced, but not necessarily more moral or more civilized.

I don't need to be Native; I have my own tribe. I am a Celt. But I am grateful for the example of First Nations people as I slowly learn to value my own identity, my own love for the earth, that came from my own ancestors.

But sometimes I have to learn that lesson from other people and other traditions. When Terry Dokis spread the labyrinth – just a truck tarp really, outlined with duct tape – in the gym, I felt a great shock of recognition. As he explained how the medicine wheel that he cherishes, and the complicated paths my own ancestors walked, fall into similar patterns, it was a moment when I felt strong enough to be who I am. A lover of trees. A listener to the messages of dreams.

I have focused, in this chapter, on the wisdom offered to us by Native traditions because it is here. We are already involved with it. It is accessible to us in our mainline churches in a way that the wisdom of, say, the ancient civilization of Samarkand is not.

The Native wisdom offered by some of our own members can make our churches strong enough to be who we are. Full of respect for Creation, strong in our community, welcoming to the physically or spiritually impoverished. And never again arrogant.

Teaching Our Successors

CHRISTOPHER WHITE

*When Esau looked up and saw the woman and children, he
said, "Who are these with you?" Jacob said, "The children
whom God has graciously given your servant."*
Genesis 33:5

"What are we to do about the children and the youth?" That has been the
constant cry since the decline in the church began in the mid-1960s. When
first the teenagers dropped out, and then the children, our churches felt like
the village of Hamelin after the Pied Piper had cleared out the young people
– grieving, wounded, and looking for answers.

When Jacob first strove with the angel, he too emerged wounded, but
blessed by his difficult encounter. Striving with God has always been hard
and we do not emerge unchanged. Yet like Jacob we can discover that we
have received not one, but multiple blessings. It's a sign of the change that
has taken place in Jacob that he doesn't claim any of the credit himself – his
wives, his children, his flocks and possessions are all a gift from God.

So too for us. Our struggles may turn out to be blessings, and those things
that we consider blessings may generate our deepest struggles.

Looking for a different model

One of our many blessings and struggles involves the role and function of Sunday school. Perhaps it's not fair to focus exclusively on the Sunday school as a vehicle for passing on our faith to our children. If our children are truly to catch our faith and run with it, what they learn in their homes, a dozen hours a day, will have far more impact than one hour a week in Sunday school. But the Sunday school is the congregation's collective effort – and with the decline of midweek church programs, it may be the congregation's only effort.

As Marva Dawn points out, in her book, *Reaching Out Without Dumbing Down*,[1] churches used to have a whole infrastructure of programs to lead children to Christian adulthood. In most denominations, these have faded. Only Sunday school – and possibly a youth group – are left. This puts more pressure than ever on Sunday morning to communicate the Christian story.

The church school, historically, has been based on the model of the school classroom. There are, of course, good reasons for that. Churches were always in the forefront of literacy. Education was a driving force in the church's history. The church provided the teachers and the subjects. We began the classrooms, and so it is hardly surprising that we would retain that model for educating our children in the stories of the faith. Indeed, when Robert Raikes first founded Sunday schools, in England, about 1780, they didn't teach religion at all. Raikes was so upset by the lawless behavior of children on Sundays – the only day off they had from their jobs in factories and mines – that he organized classes to teach them conventional subjects, largely to keep them off the streets.

But the traditional classroom model has some inherent problems. Our historical response may not be the best model in the future.

Two years ago, my congregation started to notice a loss in our Sunday school attendance. Boys in particular were missing. Parents were having more and more problems getting boys to attend church. The reason was simple – they were bored.

Our Sunday school program has traditionally been very strong, a big draw for folks in our community. We have 200 children registered, but we were certainly not getting that on a Sunday anymore. This worried me greatly.

When I acknowledged, as part of a sermon, that the educational model we were using was not responding to the children's needs, I could literally hear a whispered "yes" from the parents. I could see heads nod up and down in agreement.

Anne Lamott in her book *Traveling Mercies* speaks of the difficulties of getting her son to church.

What young boy would rather be in church on the weekends than hanging out with a friend? …You might think, noting the bitterness, the resignation, that he was being made to sit through a three-hour Latin mass. Or you might wonder why I make this strapping, exuberant boy come with me most weeks, and if you were to ask, this is what I would say: "I make him because I can, I outweigh him by more than 75 pounds."[2]

The problem lies in her final sentence. What on earth is she going to do when *he* outweighs *her* by 75 pounds? Clearly there is something lacking in her church experience – and ours – that needs to be urgently addressed. There needs to be some way of making the whole educational experience less of a trial and more a pleasure.

There's a lion in my lap!

A couple of years ago I had a conversation with my eldest daughter Sarah. For ten years, she had been attending church almost every Sunday. Out of curiosity, I named a number of what I considered to be well-known biblical stories, from Ruth to Daniel to Jonah. To my dismay, she did not know any of them. In fact, it turned out, she knew very few of the core stories of the Bible. My own daughter was in danger of becoming a biblical illiterate.

To say I was concerned would be an understatement. If the minister's daughter doesn't know the biblical stories, how can the children who come once or twice a month at best?

I shared my concerns with some others. We thought there must be another way of presenting the story, a way that would grab the children's attention and imprint it upon their hearts. We gathered together a group of concerned parents and Sunday school teachers and created a series on the story of Daniel. The key story in Daniel, in my mind, was the dramatic reversal of expectations when Daniel was tossed into the lions' den and emerged unscathed. For two special Sundays, we would focus on that story. We brainstormed games, activities, and ways of telling, showing, and experiencing the story.

Years before, I had begun a tradition in Westminster church of a Christmas Eve youth play with live sheep and goats. The congregation at first considered me a little strange for suggesting this, but we now have to turn people away on Christmas Eve because the Inn has no more room.

"If sheep work on Christmas Eve as a way to make the story of Jesus' birth real to people," I wondered, "what could we do about Daniel and the lions?"

Two weeks ahead, I told the congregation that a "special" guest was going to help us learn about Daniel and the lion's den. They nodded. I reminded them that I was the guy who brought in the live sheep. Mildly nervous laughter filled the church. I heard comments like, "He wouldn't really bring a live lion into the sanctuary would he?" That was closely followed by, "Yeah, he would."

Two weeks later, with the support of the congregation's governing board (not unanimous support, but close) our "guest" arrived. The church was packed. Animal trainer Bob Fiset brought out Pasha, the lion cub, a few weeks old, covered in tawny gold fur, and making a noise that could best be described as a cross between a purr and a growl. Bob talked to us about lions and Daniel.

I asked him, "Knowing what you know about lions, could this story have actually happened?"

He hesitated for a moment. Then he said, "If the lions accepted you in their family group, it's possible...but I wouldn't recommend trying it!"

The children and their parents were entranced. But more, from an educational viewpoint, they were able to go beyond the immediate experience with Pasha to discuss the meaning of the story. The children and their parents remember that story to this day.

I'm not recommending a constant parade of wildlife as a means of meeting the Christian education needs of our children. But the experience raised a number of issues for me. How do different individuals learn? How do different ages learn? How do different genders learn?

I know that I learn best myself through action, discussion, and interplay with others. Sitting still at a table is torture for me. At regional church meetings, monthly or annual, I'm almost always on the move. Yet others are quite content to sit through the whole meeting.

So how do we recognize, understand, and meet the different learning needs in our congregations?

The notion of Multiple Intelligences

Here's what Howard Gardner, author of *The Theory of Multiple Intelligences,* has to say about learning styles:

Humans have evolved over thousands or millions of years into different kinds of problem solvers and problem finders…and you have to understand that process if you want to figure out how people learn and how they develop and what they can and can't do.[3]

Gardner is a cognitive psychologist, researcher, and educator at Harvard University. In his work with children, and with persons with brain damage, he began to identify a fatal flaw in the way that intelligence is conventionally defined.

What I became impressed with over and over again in this work was that individuals have very jagged cognitive profiles. You will find the children are very strong in music or in language, very strong in drawing or in dance. One strength simply does not relate to how they are going to be in other cognitive areas.[4]

In other words, people have different strengths and abilities. This thesis led Gardner to identify eight major "Intelligences":[5]

- **Logical/Mathematical:** Sensitivity to and capacity to discern logical or numerical patterns; ability to handle long chains of reasoning.
- **Verbal/Linguistic:** Sensitivity to the sounds, rhythms, and meanings of words; sensitivity to the different functions of language.
- **Musical/Rhythmic:** Abilities to produce and appreciate rhythm, pitch, and timbre; appreciation of the forms of musical expressiveness.
- **Visual/Spatial:** Capacities to perceive the visual spatial world accurately, and to perform transformations on one's initial perceptions.
- **Bodily/Kinesthetic:** Ability to control one's body movements and to handle objects skillfully.
- **Interpersonal:** Capacity to discern and respond appropriately to the moods, temperaments, motivations, and desires of other people.
- **Intrapersonal:** Access to one's own feelings, and the ability to discriminate among them and draw upon them to guide behavior; knowledge of one's own strengths, weaknesses, desires, and intelligences.
- **Naturalist:** The human ability to recognize and categorize plants, animals, and natural objects of one's environment.

While this list may appear abstract, it is in fact quite sensible. We all know the little girl who stands up in church to dance to the hymns, hers is a bodily kinesthetic with an obbligato of musical. The little boy who loves to talk and write, whose questions can drive you slightly mad, is linguistic with subordinate clause of interpersonal. We all know the careful builder whose craft has perfectly folded edges, who colors within the lines, and shows perfect organizational abilities; she's spatial with a side of logical mathematical. Occasionally we encounter the reflective child who keeps analyzing his motivations and attitudes — intrapersonal. The list is actually common sense. It tells us what, on one level, we already know.

Unwilling to break out of old molds

Many Sunday schools still tend to mimic the weekday classroom that children experience, and not always for the better. For generations, the children have sat at tables, chairs, get a quick Bible story, a discussion of the meaning of the story, then a craft that may or may not be related, all in about 40 minutes.

Recent curriculums, such as *The Whole People of God*, currently the most popular Sunday school curriculum in Canada, have made great strides in encouraging teachers to get the children away from tables, to get them involved in dramatic ways. When *The Whole People of God* first came out, I worked very hard to have it used in my congregation. We have used it every year since then. It caught a wave critical to the churches' needs. But even *The Whole People of God* has its shortcomings – not least of which is the unwillingness of many teachers to let go of traditional methods.

The Whole People of God endorses the principle of Gardner's "intelligences" – that we all have different ways of learning. But I have seen too many Sunday schools that ignore them, and teachers who try to educate children the same way they were educated.

And I'm no longer convinced that a central plank in *The Whole People of God*'s platform – matching lessons to the lectionary used in worship – is still a strength. It does mean that children and adults are more likely to be hearing and learning about the same scripture passages. But at the same time, by restricting ourselves to that format, we create a biblical canon within the canon theologically, and place unnatural restrictions upon ourselves educationally.

Rigid adherence to the lectionary makes it difficult for insecure teachers to connect the Bible to current events. Skilled teachers can adapt almost any text to bring in current concerns; unskilled teachers won't risk deviating from the formula laid out for them. In the lectionary cycle, the story of Jesus speaking to the Samaritan woman at the well comes up on only one Sunday every three years. As I write these words, bombs are falling in Kosovo. (By the time you read this, it might be in Kashmir, or Turkey, or…) "Ethnic cleansing" is again a horrifying daily occurrence. Imagine the power of portraying Jesus as an Albanian going into a Serbian village and talking to the Serbian woman at the well. That's a story we need to hear today, not once in three years when it shows up in the lectionary cycle. And if a child happens to be away that Sunday, it could be six years, or nine, or never.

With such minimal exposure, how will children ever get to know that story in their hearts?

Over and over

Neil MacQueen struggled with similar issues, as the new Minister of Christian Education at the Presbyterian Church in Barrington, Illinois, in June 1990. He wanted to bring the stories alive, to interest both children and teachers.

Barrington Presbyterian sits almost in the shadow of Willow Creek, the original megachurch. Its Sunday school was in crisis. There were few teachers and fewer children. So Neil and his colleagues started from scratch. They asked one simple question: "If we were to invent Sunday school, what would it look like?"

He was determined to avoid the status quo. "Most Sunday schools are based on the 'cough syrup' premise – it tastes bad but it's good for you," Neil told me in a telephone interview.[6] "Children grow up and get out as soon as possible, and they don't come back as adults. If all the baby boomers who were in Sunday school in the 1960s came back as adults, our churches would be packed. But they didn't, in part because they were not going to expose their children to what they endured in Sunday school."

He was also determined to avoid the lectionary: "After 30 years, all it has given us is biblically illiterate congregations," he snorts scornfully.

So he and his team got together. But as they dreamed, they had to keep certain realities in mind.

First, children no longer attend regularly. How do you reach a child who only attends once every three to five weeks?

Second, finding teachers is a challenge. Like their students, teachers have other commitments. Work and family take time. They find it difficult to give the commitment that a previous generation could. Our whole social culture has shifted. Both parents work out of the home; there are longer commutes; longer hours are expected at the office. Add the realities of single parents, blended families with complex custody arrangements, and the multiplicity of other activities, and the challenge becomes almost overwhelming.

So Neil and his ministerial colleague Melissa Armstrong-Hansche made up a wish list:

1. A real art room to get messy in, taught by someone who knew real art. Modeling clay, paints, art stools not chairs, and no construction paper! Projects themselves tell the biblical story. Making the art is the lesson, not an add on.

2. A drama and puppet theatre filled with costumes and props where the children can act out the different characters of the story. By doing this they enter into the story itself and the Bible becomes real to them.

3. A Sunday school modeled on the way children enjoy learning – through movement, smells and tastes, visual stimulation, feelings, games, and drama.

4. Church leaders, parents, teachers, and congregation members who realize the importance of Sunday school to the health of the whole church.

They came up with what they called the Rotation Model[7] of Sunday school. It's based on a simple concept – teach the same story, over and over, for a four- or five-week period, but teach it a different way each Sunday. A child who comes every Sunday will know that story thoroughly, without getting bored, because the approach changes each week. A child who comes only once will still at least be exposed to the story. At the same time, the system reduces pressure on teachers to prepare fresh lessons each week.

There is an art workshop, a drama and puppet workshop, an audio-visual workshop, a Bible skills and games workshop, a music workshop, and a Bible computer lab.

When they taught a rotation about Paul, for example, they set up a small room decorated as a prison cell. Paper drop cloths were painted and hung on the walls and ceilings. Straw lay on the floor, and a Roman guard stood at the door, dialoguing with the students in character. The children who entered the cell got a true appreciation both for Paul's courage and for what members of the early church endured for their faith.

This model also is perfectly adapted to Howard Gardner's "multiple intelligences." As Neil and Melissa put it:

We now have very few discipline problems compared with the old days of sedentary curriculum. Nobody wants to miss out on the neat stuff. Workshops capture and direct their energies rather then battle against them. Classroom activities allow them to wiggle and squirm, get up and move around… We now have kids waking their parents up on Sunday mornings so they can get to church! [8]

Connecting to children's experiences

Leslee Alfano, part of the ministry team at First United in Port Credit, Ontario, has similarly struggled with the task of bringing the biblical story to life in a meaningful and current way since the early 1980s. Like MacQueen, she is concerned that we are "educating people right out of the church." [9] Her response has been to develop her own educational model that focuses on the spiritual journey of our young people. She calls it the "Story Circle."

Physically, her process does not significantly differ from the recommendations of programs such as *The Whole People of God.* She moves children off the chairs and out from the tables. Instead, they sit in circles on pieces of liturgically colored carpet: purple for Lent, red for Pentecost. This gives the children a sense of the liturgical year.

However, Leslee's real emphasis is on relationships and building community. Each session spends time on the children's experiences in the week, which Leslee ties into the Bible story. To build trust and community, they might pass a balloon around while each child in turn responds to a question. A new group might start off by asking "What's your favorite dessert?" Then perhaps, "What was your best day?" and progressively to "What gives you joy?" Each question leads the child deeper into community and builds trust.

The focus of each session is a biblical story. Instead of feeling locked into the liturgical themes of the lectionary, the Story Circle emphasizes series. To maintain a continuing link between worship and Sunday school, First United's ministry team works together to ensure that the children will learn about the Lord's Prayer or the meaning of sacraments at the same time these are covered in the sanctuary.

This system allows the flexibility to let current concerns become the basis for teaching. When the much-loved organist at First United contracted terminal cancer, her death was a blow to the whole congregation. She had known the children through both the Sunday school and the junior choir. To help the children deal with their grief, the team quickly created a series on grief for children.

The older children used the Beatitudes – "Blessed are you that mourn" – as the biblical story to frame their grief. Colors offered a metaphor to help the children express their emotions. Stories brought the feeling of loss to the surface. One story told of a boy who broke his best friend's most treasured possession. Teachers then dialogued with the children: "How would the boy who broke it feel? How would the boy feel whose treasure was broken? How would you feel if you were one of them?" So that the experience was more than merely verbal, the children chose colored circles to stand on, matching the color to their feelings.

Younger children took the Parable of the Lost Sheep. Simpler questions – "How would the sheep feel? How would the shepherd feel?" – helped these children identify their sadness.

To make sure the biblical stories don't slip quickly out of memory, First United's Sunday school takes time. They recognized that the story of Moses, for example, couldn't be rushed through. They took six weeks for it – acting it out, using movement, music, games, and physical creativity.

Leslee's methods encourage the children to actually live the story – sometimes with unexpected results. Last Lent, the children were acting out the story of Jesus' arrest and Peter's denial. When the child playing Peter was challenged about knowing Jesus, he kept saying "Yup! I know him!"

Leslee tried to insist that the boy should say, "No, I don't know him." "You're playing Peter," she explained. "Your role is to deny Jesus."

Three times she had to make this explanation. Finally the boy, with great pain in his voice, asked, "How could a friend of Jesus let him down like that?"

That is a child who has taken the story into his heart.

Leslee Alfano is an inspired teacher, a skilled facilitator, and a knowledgeable scholar. "Church school is not a numbers game," she reminded me, when I asked about results. But she admitted that average attendance had gone from 16 to 80 in six years.

Much of the success of the Story Circle depends on Leslee's own abilities. The average congregation may not have such a person available, but any congregation can apply her principles to improve the quality of teaching. A child from their Sunday school visited another church. He reported with horror in his voice, "They made us sit the whole time at tables!"

Using computers, too

One of the key elements of any Sunday school program in coming years will be a computer lab. For many Sunday schools, this will be a radically new concept. I consider it absolutely critical for the future. Children today take computers for granted. Computers are part of their lives at home, at school, and at play. Not to have them in Sunday school is to brand ourselves outdated, an anachronism.

So this past year, Westminster United introduced computers into our Sunday school for the first time. I must admit that there was some concern expressed at first. There is a value judgment associated with computers that doesn't apply to other technology, like crayons and construction paper. There is the suggestion that by using computers that the church has "sold out" to secular technology, for example. That we have been seduced by the siren call of the technological world. Or, sometimes, that the kids will just use the computers to play games, or worse, to search the Internet for pornography.

Yet similar arguments are not made about telephones and photocopiers and fax machines. All of these are tools. So are computers. Simply tools – not implements of some kind of Evil Empire. Few churches could function without these tools in their offices.

The computer lab is a part of the Sunday school. It is not the whole program. If all you do is plunk kids in front of a monitor for 40 minutes, then the tool is being misused. If however, the tools are properly integrated, the results can be quite wonderful. For the first time in living memory, I watched as parents literally had to drag their sons home after church. Both boys and girls love the computers and the biblical software, but they strike a chord with boys especially, in a way that has never happened before. "Mom, I want to stay here; this is cool!" are not words little boys tend to utter in church basements. But I hear them now. And based on others' experience, the novelty does not wear off, if these tools are used appropriately.

The computer software currently available comes mainly from conservative churches and publishers. That fact speaks volumes about the failure of the liberal mainline churches to accept and use a technology that is already changing the world. Computer software for religious education will be found mainly in the so-called "Christian bookstores." But that should not disqualify it. After all, the Bible itself can be pretty conservative. The *Alpha* program for adult education starts with a conservative viewpoint, but has been successfully used in many liberal congregations. So it's important to have a teacher present while the software is being used, to give the student guidance and interpretation in understanding the material.

Church needs come first

At Westminster, we are now putting together a trial run of the Rotation Model for our Sunday school, using Neil MacQueen's outline, for our study on Moses and the Ten Commandments. We are starting by gathering costumes, and supplies needed for an art workshop, which will include clay, but no construction paper. And I'm ordering the appropriate software.

I'm also considering placing a tent inside our basement – or maybe outside, as we'll be running this rotation before the weather gets too cold. Putting it up in the basement presents problems. Our space is multiple use and limited. Others use the space during the week. When I raised this with Neil, he challenged me: "Let the church, not the [weekday] tenants define how the basement looks. Put a tent up! Cover your dividers with art. Use stage flats. Cover the walls in pictures!"

Essentially, he told me that a church should be first of all a church – it shouldn't allow other users to define how it functions.

Today, tomorrow, and yesterday

Whether you use Neil MacQueen's Rotation Model or any other model, it is clear that the future of children's religious education will be based on story. Every church-based publisher, from what I can see, now recognizes that reality.

Lectionary based curriculums played an important role in church development. They gave us a sense of the liturgical year and a broader understanding of church. I would not want to move totally away from the lectionary, for there is a built in discipline to it that I like and need. It prevents me from preaching only about my favorite texts. It forces me to wrestle – like Jacob at the Jabbock River – with biblical passages that I would otherwise prefer to avoid.

But I am increasingly recognizing that the lectionary was a construct of the church. The *adult* church. No, more – the adult *male* church. It was not structured to take into account the new attendance patterns, or the busyness of children's lives. It was a response to the needs of the Christian church in the 1960s. As we head into the new millennium, we need to respond to our own times and challenges.

What I want to do is add to the lectionary. I want themes that let me move away from the rigidity of the lectionary – *The Whole People of God* calls their supplemental themes "modules" – while still ensuring that adults in church and children in Sunday school hear the same scripture passages. I want materials that develop Old Testament and New Testament stories over several weeks, to work these stories deeply into the consciousness of both children and adults.

I don't care whether the materials for such an approach come from *The Whole People of God,* from Neil McQueen or Leslee Alfano, or from any other source. I care only that the materials, and the teaching methods they encourage, reach our kids today.

For three years, I have volunteered a week of my time to serve as chaplain at a church camp. My teaching time was a series of 45-minute "God chats" that I had with each group of campers. I used games, stories, music, and other activities to teach them about Jonah, Joseph, Moses, and the parables of Jesus.

It was a rich and challenging (not to mention exhausting!) experience. The children ranged in age from 8 to 15. Some had extensive church exposure; some had none.

Those three years taught me two important lessons. First, teaching the faith takes great energy. We must constantly adapt our material to fit the emerging circumstances. Second, we need to invest more in our children. Over the past decades, when finances got squeezed, we let camps and other kids' organizations wither away. We need to reinvest in these important components of our ministry with children and youth. If we are serious about this ministry, we have to equip our congregations with the tools to do the job, and do it well.

It's commonly said that children are the church of tomorrow. That's not true – they are an integral part of the church today. But they will not be around tomorrow, if our congregations persist in using yesterday's methods to educate them.

Welcome Strangers

DONNA SINCLAIR

*But Esau ran to meet him, and embraced him,
and fell on his neck and kissed him, and they wept.*
Genesis 33:4

*But Mary stood weeping outside the tomb. As she wept, she
bent over to look into the tomb; and she saw two angels in
white, sitting where the body of Jesus had been lying, one at the
head and the other at the feet. They said to her,
"Woman, why are you weeping?"
She said to them, "They have taken away my Lord,
and I do not know where they have laid him."
When she said this, she turned around and saw Jesus
standing there, but she did not know it was Jesus. Jesus said to
her, "Woman, why are you weeping?
Whom are you looking for?"
Supposing him to be the gardener, she said to him,
"Sir, if you have carried him away, tell me where you have laid
him and I will take him away."
Jesus said to her, "Mary."*

> *She turned and said to him in Hebrew, "Rabouni"*
> *(which means Teacher).*
> John 20:11–16

Mary didn't recognize Jesus at first – she thought her beloved teacher was a stranger. Mary's belated recognition of Jesus holds a truth for us in the church – sometimes those we have thought of as strangers may turn out to be our finest teachers. And sometimes it isn't until we are in crisis that we are able to hear what they have to say.

It's a bit like Jacob again, frightened of what tomorrow will bring, struggling with the unfamiliar. Only after a suitable interval of wrestling with that unknown (something most of us have endured in one form or another) does he receive a blessing, a new name, and the renewed love of his brother.

Like many in the mainline churches, I have been taught much by those from far away. I owe my contacts with them to the institutional church, which sometimes brings them to us, and sometimes lets us go to them. Women in bright dresses from Africa talk about their lives, letting us see the similarities to our own, when governments begin to cut back social programs in response to the demands of what is hazily known as the world economy. Asian Christians give us a glimpse of their spirituality. South African Christians help us struggle with the meaning of forgiveness, out of their own powerful attempts to reconcile all the players from their damaged history.

Nothing has shaped us more, though, than the ideas and emotions that flow from the tiny neighboring countries of Central America – so close to us in the North, and so hurt by our cheerful presumption that cheap bananas and cheap coffee are our birthright. They know how Esau felt, when Jacob stole the blessing that should have been his.

Unexpected blessings

In 1989, for example, in the midst of a civil war in El Salvador, I was part of a church fact-finding trip to that country. This was not unusual. Church delegations were very much part of those years. Mainline North American denominations were keeping constant pressure on their own governments, noisily complaining about U.S. military aid that helped to keep brutal dictators in business.

I embarked on that trip prepared to observe, from a safe emotional distance, the marks of war, the hurt people. But one day, in an Episcopal church in San Salvador, our little group had lunch with a young woman. Mirtala Lopez had not come to the church to lobby us for any cause. She had come to see a doctor. She had been imprisoned for four months because of her work with internal refugees. Her quiet description of what she had endured seared itself into our hearts. And from her I learned – only a little, I'm still trying – that courage and stamina are essential ingredients of faith.

Another day, we sat with people from a Base Christian Community in the same city, whose Bible study was a crucial part of their lives. From these Roman Catholics, I (a Protestant through and through) learned that the Bible belongs to *us*. Not to the past, not to the scholars, but to *us*, the people who hold it in our hands and measure our own lives with it.

Neither my faith nor my relationship with scripture has been quite the same since. Many members, of many North American churches, have had similar experiences. They gather in forums in their own churches to hear a guest, or they travel to other countries to listen and learn, and they are changed by the stories of strangers.

The visit to El Salvador took place in 1989, only a year after my own denomination had agreed not to exclude homosexual people from ordination. This debate had ignited a small institutional civil war in our congregations – not as lethal as the one in Central America, but just as full of passionate, polarized conviction.

In the next few years the notion that I could grasp scripture for myself – that in fact, I was responsible for thinking and feeling my own way into what the Bible had to tell me – became very important. So did the idea that faith demands stamina and courage.

Hearing the stranger

This capacity to listen to the strangers, and allow them to touch and change our faith, is a sign of maturity in any church. It's an ability not easily acquired, because it requires humility.

For a long time, like most churches with roots in colonial power, my denomination didn't know how to listen. We believed we knew best – for the nation, for the people within our congregations, for mission fields overseas. "A great engine of righteousness" was the term historian John Webster Grant used[1] to describe the self-image of the United Church when it was founded in 1925, for example. It was ready to sweep across the nation, transforming it.

Transforming the nation wasn't a bad idea. It's just that it lacked humility. All four historic mission churches in Canada – Anglican, Methodist, Presbyterian, and Roman Catholic – all thought they knew what was best for Native children, for instance. They should become indistinguishable from those Canadians whose ancestors had come from Europe. Out of that arrogance grew the evil of the residential schools that I described in **Blessing 5, Partners in Spirituality**.

Despite the many great works they accomplished, in psychological terms the Christian churches of that era had little concept of their own shadow – the dark side of our feelings of being saintly.

Individuals who cannot see their own shadow think they are entirely good. They project all their inconvenient hatreds and flaws (particularly those failings of which they are least aware) safely out onto others. We all do this; and we can often catch ourselves at it if we note that we are irrationally angry with someone. So-and-so is too busy, I complain to myself; she's always rushing past me, ignoring me or making demands on me – just when I am desperately busy myself.

The same syndrome operated on a collective level with the churches. Other people needed reforming, they thought, others needed to be civilized and educated. At the same time, these Christian institutions were convinced of their own brightness and innocence, until one day – like Mary – they peered into the darkness and were shocked to discover that their mission had gone awry. Native people had begun to explain that the loss of their own culture (as a way of dealing with massive change) was too high a price to pay. They began to describe how enormously many of them had suffered in the residential schools.

Although many from the First Nations had become Christian, a crucial aspect of mission had failed. Instead of caring for the children – the very thing Jesus tells us is absolutely necessary[2] – we had hurt them.

As churches, at last we were forced to begin to own our own darkness – the pride that had made us believe we knew what was best for others.

The shadow side

In the same way, over a period of years and conflict and pain and study, some churches slowly began to look into the darkness of their own attitudes toward gays and lesbians. Some members began to see that Christendom had confined gay people to a ghetto, as surely as an earlier church had confined Jews and slaves to ghettoes. By focusing attention on a few rules, a few out of many, a few that made sense mainly in the context of an ancient culture, they had blinded themselves to the gospels' central theme, to "love one another."

At the same time, some Christians began to rethink the hostile portrait of the Pharisees that they had been taught earlier in scripture. They were reminded that Jesus was a Jew, and painfully began to seek out the roots of anti-Semitism within their faith.

All this has forced some Christian churches to struggle with their sense of infallibility. Usually, they have come out wiser. In the study of scripture provoked by the debate over gay ordination, in the re-interpretation of scripture passages that have fed Christian anti-Semitism, in scenes evoked in courtrooms by the bitter memories of those who were children in Indian residential schools, we have begun to acknowledge our shadow side.

And as we do, we find some measure of wholeness. We recognize that we are three-dimensional – we are more than cardboard cutouts with no depth, with only one side, always turned to face the sun. The Christian churches are not perfect. We are, collectively, the same living mixture of saint and sinner that makes up every human.

And we are beginning to recognize our new teachers: the ones we had wronged. It's not so far from the urge that drove Jacob home to be reconciled with the brother he had hurt – an urge born out of maturity, perhaps, or homesickness, or even love.

There is much to learn. But the churches' ability to survive into the next century is in direct proportion to their capacity to know and accept their own shadow. The energy that has been spent denying our imperfections needs to be freed and turned to healing the world.

The very soul of the church

I am overwhelmed with sharp unease – no, panic is a better word – whenever a church growth expert points out that the churches that are most successful in numerical growth don't do a great deal of social justice.

In the late 20th century, according to author William Easum, many congregations focused on "humankind's physical needs almost to the exclusion of their spiritual needs." Now, with a swing to what he calls "paradigm communities," he says candidly that "the danger...is that the pendulum might swing in the other direction, and paradigm communities might concern themselves only with getting people ready to meet God."

He describes how, in his Colonial Hills church, "over a ten-year period, several hundred active members joined other congregations because they did not believe their pastor and laity should be involved in the root causes of social justice."

To his credit, he says that even when people walked out because of a peace conference or work in community organizing, "We continued to be faithful to the gospel."[3]

I believe that Jesus' various calls – to love one another, to feed my lambs, to remember that the poor are blessed – are the very soul of the Christian church. And I believe we are slowly (we are still infants at this, I know) learning how to do it. Out of humility, not triumphalism and pride. Humility underpinned with prayer. With such a clear sense of our own human weakness that we will listen hard for God. And with a knowledge that God likes to dwell with those who are in pain, the strangers.

Of all the distinguishing marks of the Christian church, the moments when we have found ourselves companioning the voiceless and marginalized may be the most important. This is what transforms us as a church. Whenever we have the courage to walk and talk and listen to the strangers among us – as many denominations do with refugees or prisoners or the impoverished – we see the Christ. In their resurrection, we will discover our own. Our relationships with those "others" – the people we hurt in the residential schools, the people who left the church over gay ordination, the Japanese citizens Canada deported or interned without trial, the draft dodgers some North Americans vilified, and, yes, the bald eagles we almost killed off with our toxins – all these relationships are not over and done with, sealed safely in the past, but dynamic and ongoing.

Beyond our battles

We don't know how these continuing relationships will change us. We are on the road still. By becoming a church *for* the poor and stranger, we may become a church *of* the poor and stranger. But why not? That is how we began, two millennia ago. And those whom our culture has marginalized – at home, or in the community of nations, in the Third World – who have struggled with our theologies and transformed them into their own – those can bring us renewed faith.

My husband Jim was president of the United Church's Manitou Conference the year after our denomination's bitterly fought decision that homosexual persons seeking ordination would not be barred solely on the basis of their sexual orientation. Some were wondering why anyone would even want to be ordained as a minister of this church. Between supper time and the ordination service, Jim scribbled notes for his sermon, wondering how to address a people torn by their internal wars.

He found himself gripped by a memory he had almost forgotten. A lean, elderly woman he had met on a coffee plantation, on the spine of a mountain ridge in El Salvador, "a refugee from wars in her own country," had given him and his two companions four eggs.

Why four, they had wondered, when there were only three of them?

Because that was all she had, she had replied.

So, in a voice choking with recalled emotion, the president of Conference offered the people of an embattled denomination the example of this little old woman. In a much more lethal war than ours, she was surviving with her generosity and love for others intact.

Despite "her oily black hair tied back, her skin like leather, her clothes handed up from others far away," she gave "little sense of the brokenness in her past or the pain in her present." Because she was so filled with the strength of God.

Mother Faith, he called her. For him, she was an example of the faith that is the only ground on which the people of a troubled church can meet. Like Christ, faith reaches out of the darkness to touch people who are lost and angry and operating out of unresolved deep pain. Like Christ, she is hard to recognize, a stranger, until we are ready to accept what she offers.

Rethinking our theology

Ecumenical partners can sometimes bless us with a roadmap revealing their struggle with the faith, showing us how they transformed it to suit their own context.

Witness, for instance, the great document that came out of the struggle against apartheid in South Africa. In the mid-1980s, *The Kairos Document: Challenge to the Church* appeared from a group of about 30 theologians in South Africa. It was offered to a country groaning to free itself from an economic and class system based on race.

It is a soaring document, appealing to Christians to stand with those who are oppressed, tightly arguing a position the churches can take in the struggle. Although it addresses a specific situation, its principles could be addressed to us as we face the tightening grip of large corporations on North America's soul, as companies grow larger and employees less significant:

Much of what we do in church services has lost its relevance to the poor and oppressed. Our services and sacraments have been appropriated to serve the need of the individual for comfort and security. Now these same Church activities must be reappropriated to serve the real religious needs of all the people and to further the liberating mission of God and the Church in the world. [4]

It's important to figure out what "the real religious needs of all the people" are today, and to understand what, in our country, is meant by "the liberating mission of God." The old arrogance won't do anymore.

Perhaps it means the church can offer an antidote to the downsizing trends of the day, for example. Melding two or three congregations into one unit to cut staff and save money may not always be the right answer. It may be merely copying a corporate model that has little to do with faithfulness.

Perhaps we can look carefully at how we use our buildings. Where we have not already done so, churches might find a model in the inner courtyards of churches in El Salvador, for example, where *campesina* women come to make tortillas in safety. Of course we aren't into making tortillas – certainly not outdoors in January in Canada! But churches can be places of safety. Places where battered women can drop their guard, where the hungry can eat and the homeless can sleep, where the elderly can find companionship and the young can find idealism, and those who fear can be comforted.

Most important of all – like the South African church – we can do the analysis required to rethink our theology. That has been the gift that gay candidates and clergy have brought to the church. By their willingness to stand and be named, they have initiated a long process of re-interpreting the Biblical material, rethinking the origins of sexuality for all Christians, helping us reflect so that some of the most vulnerable are not punished for being who they are.

As the South African theologians pointed out:

The present crisis has now made it very clear that the efforts of church leaders to promote effective and practical ways of changing our society have failed. This failure is due in no small measure to the fact that "Church Theology" has not developed a social analysis that would enable it to understand the mechanics of injustice and oppression.[5]

Without triumphalism

Some denominations are slowly embarking on the kind of social analysis described in that *Kairos* document. They have begun – painfully, and often at great cost – to look at history and repent.

That history may involve racism or sexism or discrimination based on sexual orientation. It could be based on education, or income. It could even be based on ideology or a particular confession of faith. The church in Canada may have an advantage here because, as a country, Canadians have never had much of the power that permits triumphalism. It was populated by successive waves of history's rejects – impoverished French, United Empire Loyalists on the wrong side of America's revolution, Irish fleeing the Potato Famine, Scots who had endured the bitterness of the Highland Clearances – and later, refugees from Vietnam, Somalia, Central America, Yugoslavia, all weary of war or hunger, and eager to turn their minds to the arts of peace.

The U.S. too has a tradition of welcoming the outcast. The oft-quoted message at the Statue of Liberty says, "Give me your tired, your poor, your huddled masses…" But with, we Canadians suspect, a different agenda. William Easum says that the United States defines itself – in his words – as the country that "will become the guardian of peace, selling its military might to protect the rest of the world. Global National Products will replace Gross National Products… A global lifestyle will emerge that involves food, travel, films fashion, language and human rights."[6]

We have had no power like that. We never will. But we remember, from our experience with the residential schools, that one culture doesn't fit all.

A former United Church moderator, the Very Rev. Sang Chul Lee, was having dinner with friends one night during the Oka crisis. He had just returned from a visit to the beleaguered Mohawk on the other side of the barricades. "The moderator," he pointed out, "has no power – but a great deal of authority."

If we can learn from our colleagues in Third World countries; and from our own members who live in a Third World of social exclusion based on race, or gender, or orientation, or economics, we will have a Christian church without power, but with the vast authority of the gospel.

The congregation and the community

In our congregations, the idea that the outcast teaches us the faith might mean that every congregation needs to know the community around it. How many single Moms live there? How many kids live in poverty? How many people are struggling with two low-paying jobs, and still can't make it? How many have no jobs, and are steadily sinking into the quicksand of depression? Who is lonely, or being beaten up, and afraid to reach out for help? Who's too sick to ask for help?

And why are these things happening? What corporate or government decisions have contributed to these situations? What can be done to change things?

It means those who can picket, picket. Those who can petition, petition. Those who can speak out without losing their jobs, speak out. Those who can form employment agencies, do so. Those who can run for political office, do so. Those who can make soup, serve it. And everybody prays.

A congregation can only sustain that kind of commitment if they are held together – no, more than that – bound together, lifted up together, by worship. They cannot do it without constantly experiencing God. A congregation needs to have Taizé services and midweek worship and prayer meetings and healing services. Every possible way that people can do the inner work is crucial to the outer work. Inner and outer go together. They must be sustained, as Mary was, sustained by a vision of the risen Christ that is so real and purposeful and sweaty that she could mistake him for a gardener.

In the national offices

All this means the national offices of denominations will continue to have a role, providing resources, vision, and care. They will not have the role they once took for themselves – to tell people what to do and believe. Rather, committed people are busy and needy, and need to rely on a body that can collect liturgy and music. Information is required too, to feed congregations that need to know how to offer sanctuary for a refugee or what corporation is harming the land. National offices can broker information and share creative resources.

National offices can also offer analysis, helping those who are head-down in details and surrounded by local problems get an overview of the situation all over the country, in the light of the gospel.

They can offer a model for activism around urban development, say; or act as broker with a list of experts to consult when there is an ethical dilemma at a local hospital; or bring in an overseas guest to provide a different perspective as catalyst.

In other words, large denominational offices need to do more of what they now often do well: provide resources, connections, and support for local congregations.

The experience of darkness

The renewal of our faith and the rebirth of the churches rests on our ability to be modest enough to learn from those we once felt we were called to teach.

It won't be easy. Henri Nouwen, in his journal of living in Latin America, published as *¡Gracias!,* describes the wisdom he gained from being with the poor. It is transferable wisdom; the encounter with poverty is as real in the food banks and welfare lines of North America as in the *barrios.* In his words,

Anyone who really becomes involved in the daily lives and struggles of the poor cannot avoid moments and periods of conflict… It can even lead to a struggle and confrontation with God, who does not seem to make [God's] presence known. Thus a spirituality marked by the struggle for liberation can lead to an experience of deep darkness, which will require true humility. It is this humility that enables us to continue in the struggle, even when we see little progress, to be faithful even when we experience only darkness, to stay with the people even when we ourselves feel abandoned.[7]

As the culture shifts and – in many congregations – attendance continues to fall, it will be easy for us to despair. If the individualism that marks our culture continues, the mainline Christian churches may feel that they "experience only darkness," in Nouwen's phrase, and "feel abandoned."

But that puts us in a touch with a new humility which – to continue Nouwen's insights – "has deep connections with the humility of Jeremiah, who confronts God in the midst of his confusion, and with the humility of John of the Cross, who stays faithful in the darkness."[8]

It has deep connections, too, with the newfound humility of Jacob. Only after a long time, shaken and visibly wounded, does this flawed character learn his new identity. It will be the same for us. We are not the only ones ever to be caught in a nighttime of struggle; and it is out of such nights that the new vision of church we have been seeking may come.

Remember Jacob. He endured, faithfully convinced of God's power to bless him, refusing to let go until that happened. The next day, Jacob humbly bows himself "to the ground seven times, until he came near his brother. But Esau ran to meet him, and embraced him, and fell on his neck and kissed him, and they wept."

We are in the midst of events very much like these. And if we refuse to let go of our faith in God – if we can remain convinced of God's power to bless us – that blessing may be ours as well.

BLESSING 8

Up Front

CHRISTOPHER WHITE

Then they came to Elim, where there were twelve springs of
water and seventy palm trees;
and they encamped there by the water.
The whole congregation of the Israelites set out from Elim, and
Israel came to the wilderness of Sin,
which is between Elim and Sinai...
The whole congregation of the people of Israel murmured
against Moses and Aaron in the wilderness.
Exodus 15:27—16:2

Jacob said to Laban,
"Send me away, that I may go to my own home
and country."
Genesis 30:25

It was nine o'clock on a Wednesday night. I was downstairs watching television when the doorbell rang. I crawled out of the couch and headed upstairs. Standing at my front door was Tim, age 17.

"Mr. White," he called out in his trademark cheerful voice, "are you doing anything right now?"

With some regret for missing an episode of *Star Trek Voyager*, I replied, "Nothing particularly pressing."

"Then let's go for a walk!" spoke this energetic teenager.

And so we went for a walk. It was late spring, a gorgeous evening. For an hour I just listened, and answered when appropriate. It was a marvelous moment in ministry. I was honored that this young man felt he could come to my door, and that he trusted me to walk with him as part of his life's journey. It was the perfect end to one of those mountaintop days that you sometimes get in my line of work.

The day had begun with the visit of a woman in her 70s who had just gone through confirmation. She had come by to thank me and handed me a letter that very graciously spoke of the difference the church had made in the course of her life. This was followed by a letter in the mail from a young adult heading off to university in the fall, who wanted to make sure that I knew how my ministry had affected her life. It was very touching and I was deeply moved.

Of course not all days are like that. For every mountaintop day, there is time in the valley. But in my years in ministry I have been fortunate that I've spent more time on the mountain than in the valley. Sadly, however, far too many clergy today find that the valley seems to be their permanent address.

But someone has to do it

Being a minister today can be tough, very tough. It may always have been difficult, but it seems particularly challenging right now. Numbers in worship are dropping in most denominations. Finances stay mired in the red or barely make it into the black As a result, people are looking for a savior or a scapegoat. "If only we could find that right minister, all our problems would be solved," goes the mantra.

Those charged with hiring or "calling" new clergy keep looking for the answer to their church's problems, at times laying expectations on their professional staff that no human could possibly meet.

On the other side, clergy can in fact be part of the problem, sticking to their way of thinking with the tenacity of any lay person clinging to the good old days and the good old ways.

This chapter is about what is going on in the lives of ministers.

Hanging on by their fingernails

I like clergy. The great majority work very hard, have tremendous faith, and care for their people and their church. Yet many of them are dispirited and not filled with the energy and hope our congregations need.

In a recent report, the Division of Ministry Personnel and Education of the United Church's British Columbia Conference told its Executive that

The general mood or sense of well-being (among clergy) was characterized as poor, low, depressed, uncertain, anxious… There is a sense that our church, our ministry, our service to the community, is not being valued, is not having any impact or influence.[1]

Last December, I was having lunch with two colleagues. By happenstance, most of the town's clergy were also there, at different tables. All of them looked completely worn out; all had tales of stress and difficulty.

Doug Goodwin of British Columbia Conference forwarded me an e-mail comment from an American colleague:

Even in the deep South, the description of clergy as those whose sense of well-being isn't being very well resonates… Much of it comes from the rapid passing (even in the Bible Belt) of anything resembling "Establishment." Did you know, for instance, that even though the Southern Baptist Convention grew in numbers in 1997, more than 2/3 of all Southern Baptist Churches lost members in that most recent statistical year? Too many of our colleagues of every American denominational stripe are doing exactly what the Canadian study suggests: hanging on by their fingernails, hoping that the whole house of cards won't collapse before they can retire and/or get the hell out.

Facing up to crisis

These vivid feelings are echoed in Robert Wuthnow's book *The Crisis in the Churches.* Wuthnow states bluntly:

Crisis is not a word pastors are fond of using. They prefer to be optimistic about their ministries. But listening to them discuss their frustrations and observing how gingerly they treat the relationship between faith and economic concerns, one gains the impression that there truly is a crisis of significant proportions in America's churches.[2]

We have, in fact, known about this crisis in the churches and among the clergy for some time. We simply have not been willing to acknowledge it. Back in 1991, in *The Once and Future Church,* Loren Mead stated

No one faces a greater challenge in the church than the clergy. In the past four decades they have already experienced more change than they expected. From being a high status/low stress profession, the clergy has become a low status/high stress profession.[3]

There have been two main responses to the crisis. One, advocated by William Chris Hobgood in *The Once and Future Pastor,* suggest renewal and redefinition. We live, he says, in "a culture of disregard, that neither opposes nor supports the church."[4] Sunday morning soccer or a myriad of other activities have equal weight with church attendance for parishioners. This leaves clergy feeling powerless and without influence. Hobgood argues for a clerical renewal based upon a recovery of the sacred, the formation of community, continual education, and a renewal of vocation.

Another voice offers quite a different vision, a return to the past. In *The Empty Church: Does Organized Religion Matter Anymore?* history professor and author Thomas Reeves argues that a return to orthodoxy will lead to a renewal of the church. He states clearly what he expects of a minister:

A pastor should have an attractive personality… He or she should learn names, social-ize, shake a lot of hands, smile a lot… Pastors should have some solid training in counseling, organizational skills, finance, and church growth. Clergy in the renewed mainline must be active for the faith. They should regularly call on parishioners; visit hospitals, nursing homes and jails; answer letters promptly; carefully prepare worship services; knock on some doors. They should study (not just read)… In no other profession except for the professorate is the temptation to be lazy as easily indulged.[5]

Reeves' job description calls for what many of us would consider im-possible qualifications. It sounds slightly like the joke going the rounds a few years ago, about the congregation that wanted a fresh young minister with at least 40 years pastoral experience!

Two possible solutions

We all know that there is a significant problem, but what to do about it?

Recently, my denomination introduced an Employee Assistance Plan for all its employees. It's a great idea. It provides counseling and other ser-vices when you need them. But let me suggest it's not enough.

There are two things I believe are desperately needed, one of which will not cost any denomination a dollar.

The first is gratitude. When was the last time a denomination said "thank you" to its clergy? In my ministry I do not remember one time when an official in my denomination ever acknowledged how difficult it is for clergy today or how much they appreciate the work that clergy do. On the contrary, clergy get bashed as the source of the church's problem, rather than being seen as integral to the solution.

Would it be so difficult for leaders to pen a thank you letter for clergy? It sounds so very simple but it would have tremendous symbolic value and give heart to those of us in pastoral ministry. Cultivating a culture of civility and support towards ministry personnel is woefully lacking in our denominational structures. It's time to change that.

The second will cost a lot more, but will improve the quality of our ministry by clearing the ranks of those who are dispirited and discouraged. There is a crying need for a decent early retirement package for clergy. It's true that many ministers do not want to retire. They have been wrapped up for so long in their work that they cannot imagine themselves in any other role, and so they will work part-time, doing pulpit supply or pastoral visitation, well into their 70s. But others, as I noted above, are just hanging on desperately until they can retire.

When teachers in Ontario were offered a good early retirement package they flocked to it in such numbers that instead of a surplus in teachers, there is now a shortage. I am quite confident that the church would have a similar experience.

I recognize that ministers are not alone in feeling stress. Teachers, people in business, those on the factory floor, the call center, or the retail sector all feel the same way. It's difficult out there for all of us.

Impossible expectations

But there are some inherent structural issues that clergy carry with them. We are, even in these modern times, seen as God's representatives in the church. When we make errors or mistakes – as we inevitably will – such flaws are viewed as failures of the church or shortcomings of the God we worship.

At times it seems that we are supposed to share in God's omniscience. We are expected to know when people are sick, wounded, hurting, or annoyed. Even if we are not told about a situation requiring our attention, we're "supposed to know."

A colleague incurred the wrath of a member of her congregation for not having visited this person's child in hospital. When this colleague protested that no one, not even the parents, had bothered to tell her that the child was having surgery, she received this terse reply: "Well, you *should* have known."

That mother never forgave the minister in question, and never returned to that church.

It's not what you know that hurts you in this business, it's what you don't know. Like a land mine, the things we fail to do may not kill our ministry, but they can certainly maim it.

Every clergyperson I know has a comparable story to tell. Being a minister today means waking up every morning knowing that someone somewhere is annoyed with you. Upset. Even angry.

Maybe it's something you said in your sermon. You were too political, or not political enough. They didn't like the joke you told, or you didn't tell enough jokes. You didn't preach enough of the Bible, or you preached too much Bible. Your theology was too liberal, or too conservative.

Or maybe they simply don't like you as a person. In fact, no matter how brilliant a preacher you are, no matter how compassionate a pastor, or faithful a visitor, someone will not like you. I guarantee that every minister reading this book can name at least one person who no longer attends that church because of him or her.

I was told of a study showing that when any preacher stands up in the pulpit that first Sunday, a certain percentage of the congregation will find something they don't like. It could be as little as the minister's laugh, or choice of shoes, or color of eyes. It doesn't matter. Put a different person in the pulpit and the same percentage (though different individuals) will experience that dislike.

I can't document the existence of such a study. It may be apocryphal. But it certainly rings true to experience. You start your first day on the job having already alienated an individual or a group of people simply by the way you smile or speak or comb your hair.

Missing persons

If you doubt this, look at the turnover in leadership or attendance when a new pastor arrives. Some people come out of the woodwork who haven't been seen in the church for years. And others just disappear.

"Why don't you visit so and so," someone will suggest. "They haven't been around much since you arrived."

I was told that in both of my last two congregations. When I visited those people, I was always received courteously. I was told that "everything was fine." But somehow, "things just weren't the same" since my predecessor left. They'd "think about coming back." They never did. Not while I was there, anyway.

I was beginning to feel slightly paranoid about members dropping out, until friends of mine followed me to a former congregation. As the years unfolded, I asked them about people I had known there.

"Who?" they replied. Or, "They haven't been around much since you left."

A minister for whom I have great respect told me, in my first year, "People come and go. As long as more come than go, everything is normal, so don't worry."

It's great advice. But I still worry.

Ray Leppard was my supervising minister when I was an intern at Kirk United Church in Edmonton, Alberta. He was a pastor in the very best sense of the word. During my time at Kirk he also gave me some excellent advice. "Christopher," he said, "in your ministry you have two choices. You can move every few years to experience change, or you can stay in one congregation for a very long time and watch the whole church change around you."

He was absolutely correct, but watching people come and go is not easy. If nothing else, it threatens my own self-esteem.

The church is a fluid community

Our congregations have historically reflected the shape of society. Churches were stable and settled places, rooted in stable and settled communities. People didn't move about much. Your parents and their parents before them attended the same place of worship. People spent 30 to 40 years in the same job and retired with a gold watch. Generations lived, had children and grand-children, and died all in the same place. The gravestones in church cemeteries tell the tale of this long-term permanence.

But now the average family moves every five years. Families are fluid. They come together, break apart, and work in different parts of the city, the country, or the world. For a time my wife and I lived in Calgary; my sister lived in London, England; my parents lived in Toronto. We were an extended family – extended all over the globe!

Following divorce or separation, children spend time with one parent, then move to the other, throwing family routines into turmoil. Add to that the complexity of commuting, where people live in one community but spend most of their time in another, and it becomes apparent that there is no such thing anymore as a traditional stable and settled community.

Unfortunately, too many congregations continue to operate on the assumption that people live, work, and have all their loyalties and commitments within a single geographical and residential area.

In actual fact, these social changes mean that churches also experience constant and fluid change. Leadership is continually being lost and renewed. That can be invigorating. It helps to prevent power blocks and old-guard cliques. But it can also be frustrating. The responsible people in the congregation often have little church memory. It can be challenging to find people who actually know what is going on in the place. Just when you develop key leaders who can share their gifts with your church, they are transferred to Nova Scotia or Colorado. People come, people go, and the ministry team is left constantly putting fractured pieces together.

There are other consequences to this – grief, for example. Clergy genuinely grieve when key lay persons move away or simply stop coming. This isn't necessarily anyone's fault – people's priorities change; church may not interest them anymore. Others stop coming because of an issue in the church at large, or because of a conflict with another personality. It's not always because of something that the minister did or did not do. Occasionally these folks will find their ways to other congregations, but usually they simply don't go anywhere else.

We're told not to take it personally, but we do; we can't help it.

Time for moving on

Clergy also grieve their losses of friends and familiar patterns when the clergy themselves move to a new congregation. Why do they do it, then?

Partly, it's historical. In the past, many denominations deliberately moved their ministers every three or four years. When we didn't have telephones and television and e-mail, it was a way of building denominational networks. It made sure that every minister knew a variety of lay people, in a variety of places – and vice versa, of course. It was also a form of continuing education; each pastor carried what he (in those days, always "he") had learned in one congregation to the next one, thus exposing them to different theologies, procedures, and ways of doing things.

Today, moves result more from wishful thinking. A new congregation is a fresh start. You haven't alienated anyone yet, nobody's mad at you, and you wonder if maybe this can be the place you were meant to be all along.

About a year ago I was contacted by a church on the West Coast. During a particularly difficult day, as the snow blew past my window, I looked at pictures of the ocean view, the boats bobbing in the harbor, and the large fish caught offshore. I fantasized about this perfect church where the tide rose on gentle faithful folk while their mildly eccentric minister/writer puttered about with a fly rod in one hand and a Bible in the other.

Of course, I knew in my heart that this was purely fantasy. That church was filled with people who had the same needs and challenges as my present congregation. But it was an inexpensive mental holiday nonetheless.

For more and more clergy, moving every few years becomes less and less of an option. Spouse and children are no longer assumed to be part of the clergy package. They have their own friends, their own careers, and they want to stay put for a long time. This can be good for the minister's family; to many people's surprise, it can also be good for the church. In the midst of rapid change, the clergy represent stability and continuity. The Alban Institute has done numerous studies showing that if a pastoral relationship changes every few years, a congregation will rarely reach its full potential. Instead of dealing with issues of congregational mission, they are constantly involved in saying hello and goodbye.

Commuter clergy

Short-term ministries are like short-term relationships. There is a continual subtext of distrust. People wonder, "How can I trust you with the secrets of my life and my heart if you are going to take off next year?" A long-term relationship allows more intimate trust to grow. The longer you are in a place – provided you remain open and impartial – the more people feel free to come to you. Clergy can become more deeply involved in the community, more part of the Christian family.

At the same time, clergy need to make sure that they remain fresh. The former pattern of moving every few years gave clergy a new audience before the old one realized their minister was stuck in a rut! Today, clergy need to be more intentional about updating themselves and not taking their church for granted. Continuing education is no longer an optional extra – it's a necessity. Long-term pastoral relationships thrive when there is continual renewal of both clergy and lay. When stagnation sets in, it can be time to honestly re-examine the future.

One growing trend that I am seeing and hearing about more often is the clergy commuter. Especially in large urban areas and their surrounding communities, the clergy family stays in the same community while the minister commutes to her or his new church. Since most of

North America commutes anyway, the minister simply shares the daily experience of his or her parishioners. Having done it myself for three years when I commuted from Calgary to Springbank, I know it can work effectively – as long as regular and predictable office hours are kept.

Exiles in unfamiliar territory

It should be obvious to anyone that the church today is not in a period of triumphal ascendancy. Some denominations are still growing, but all are falling short of their goals and expectations.

Herbert O'Driscoll thinks of the church as living through a time of exile.[6] It is in transition, isolated from its traditional space, preserving old customs and building new ones, as it waits to find out where it will settle next. The church today is the Hebrew people in Babylon, struggling to sing the Lord's song amid strangers. It is Jacob's descendants, following a wild-eyed Moses through the deserts of Sinai. It is Jacob himself, serving a foreign master in an unfamiliar land.

O'Driscoll, now retired, worked in pastoral ministry over 37 years, from 1954-1992. He has experienced both the boom and the bust of the church. He conveys his wisdom through preaching courses all over North America – including a stint as Dean of the College of Preachers in Washington, DC. Like Walter Brueggemann, he takes the Exile as the defining metaphor for the church today.

Before the exile of 587 BCE, Judaism was a highly structured religion with a priestly caste centered in Jerusalem. After the Babylonians conquered Jerusalem and drove the people into exile, the Jewish faith became fragmented. There were many voices, from Ezekiel to the author of Ecclesiastes, competing with visions for the future. The unifying story of the children of Israel, of Jacob, was in danger of disappearing.

The parallel to our present experience came to O'Driscoll in a flash of insight 20 years ago. At an ordination service in the mid-1970s, he looked at an ordinand and said: "I am the old Jew who remembers Jerusalem before the Babylonians came. You are the young Jew who was born in Babylon. It is your task to rebuild the city into something new."

Misleading statistics

"But," I asked O'Driscoll, "what about all the statistics that more than 80 percent of North Americans still call themselves Christian?"

Such statistics tell us more about the question than the answer, O'Driscoll suggests: "We get tricked by language. A pollster asks you during dinner time if you consider yourself to be a Christian, and you say yes. The pollster doesn't ask what you believe as a Christian, or if there is any faith substance to your answer."

Terry Finlay, the Anglican Bishop of the Diocese of Toronto, echoes O'Driscoll's caution. "We're talking about apples and oranges when pollsters ask people that question," he told me.[7]

I thought of people I know who would without hesitation describe themselves as Christians, but who haven't been to a church or expressed their faith in decades. If the question were, "Are you an active participating Christian?" the numbers would be more likely to reflect church attendance figures, currently at around 30 percent. Statistics of church attendance show attendance declining by about 50 percent for each successive generation. Attendance is dropping faster in the liberal mainline churches than in conservative churches, but the trend affects all churches.

Bishop Finlay has experienced the depth of that change during his ministry. "My predecessor used to pick up the phone and call the premier of the province. He'd suggest that they meet for a cup of tea, and the two of them would discuss government issues of concern to the church." Today, the Anglican church usually speaks to government either as part of an interdenominational group or, increasingly, as an interfaith coalition.

These social changes have affected Anglican priests to such an extent that one told Terry, "The church I was trained for is not the church that I'm in." One of my own professors, at seminary in the 1980s, admitted in an unguarded moment that the faculty no longer had any idea what kind of church they were training their students for.

And the pace of change keeps accelerating. The church you were called to a few years ago has already been superseded by the one you minister to today, and that same church will be completely different again in five years. As clergy, we have to constantly adapt and change. What worked 12 months ago might be totally inappropriate now. It's like tap dancing on quicksand. The ground beneath you keeps shifting; if you stop moving, you're sunk.

The glory days of Christendom have ended. Christians are a minority people.

Longing for the past

Yet we continue to work in churches that cling to memories of the recent past. Herbert O'Driscoll picks up another biblical image – of Elim, the oasis visited by the Israelites in the desert. "My generation all have a memory of Elim," he says. "It's sometime in the late '50s or early '60s, the kids are in the station wagon, hamburgers cost 25 cents, one income supports the family, and there's a new house in the suburbs." The church was always full. Youth groups flourished. There was never a lack of people to serve on committees.

Like the people of Israel, no one likes to abandon Elim. It was a wonderful place. And when you have to move on, you get mad, and start murmuring. In Sinai, they murmured against Moses and Aaron. Today, suggests O'Driscoll, the clergy become the focus of their anger. The church has had to leave Elim behind, and someone has to pay the price.

Model for an altered mindset

Memories of packed buildings can make life awfully difficult for the current incumbents. I asked Herb O'Driscoll how ministers cope in this new world.

"The church is not an organization, it is an organism," he told me.

His statement crystallized much of what I have been struggling with over the last few years. In our churches, we have an organizational structure. But we don't have an organism plan. We know how to tinker with the machinery; we don't know how to promote the health of a mystical body. That's why we find past and future continually in conflict. Organisms grow, and change. I am not the same person I was five years ago, nor am I now the person I will be in five years. The same is, and will be, true for my church.

So how can ministers equip themselves so they do not become part of the ever growing statistics on long term disability? I asked this question of both Bishop Finlay and Herbert O'Driscoll.

"There is a neurotic anger toward all institutions – politicians, corporations and the church – and clergy get caught in that," O'Driscoll explained. Like people who work for a corporation that is undergoing massive restructuring, clergy have to learn that this earthquake is not their fault, not a personal failure.

Clergy have to change their mental images, he continued. They have been entrusted with an organism, not an organization. The parenting analogy works reasonably well here. Just as children develop their own unique personalities, so do congregations. A responsible parent or minister can nurture and guide, but can never totally control the development of that organism.

He suggested, "Find an older colleague you can integrate into the church's ministry so that that person can be a lightning rod for the anxiety of older folk who still yearn for Elim."

Terry Finlay has pastoral care responsibilities for hundreds of clergy. For him, the important thing is to "nurture the faith that sustains us in times of trial. Find yourself a spiritual director who can guide you through the stresses facing the church today." He also recommends a disciplined use of time – not only for work, but for spouse and children, and for study of the scriptural foundations of faith. Combined with prayer and meditation, these give clergy a solid grounding to carry them through times of deep stress.

As ministers we tend to gravitate to those in the congregation who support us. But perhaps we neglect the value of those who disagree. Michael

Fullan wrote an article on education called "Emotion and Hope: Constructive Concepts for Complex Times."

*The role of enthusiasts has been overestimated, and the value of resisters, on the other
hand, has been under-appreciated… Finding a way to reconcile positive and negative
emotion is the key to releasing energy for change.*[8]

The people who want to go back to Elim may be the ones who can
help us find the next oasis. Clergy need to use their emotional intelligence
to help lead the churches to the next level.

But we are confused about what is expected of us today.

Team, team, team

In spite of our current challenges, there are many wonderful attributes to
contemporary ministry. I cannot think of a more exciting and challenging
time to be in the church. We do not have to feel defeated; we can make this
into a time of opportunity and growth.

One of the keys to a healthy ministry, wherever we are, whatever the
size of our congregations, is to realize that we are in a team ministry. We are
not lone wolves. We are in a team with the people in our congregations,
with colleagues in our own churches, and with colleagues in the other
churches and other faiths.

In the past there could be a tendency to competition and even jeal-
ousy between ministerial colleagues and neighboring congregations. That
trend is beginning to change. I see the evidence of that in my own community. My church, Westminster United, is in Whitby, a town of over 70,000
people. Whitby has three United churches, each unique and different. Over
the years we have evolved into what we refer to as a "cluster." We work
together, while maintaining our own unique identity. As clergy, we meet
regularly to share concerns and offer each other support. We also plan
joint workshops and events on everything from stewardship to Sunday
school and worship.

By working together, we build trust among all of us. So when there is occasional "migration," (sheep heading to another pasture) between the churches, we don't get defensive or protective of our "turf." Instead, we understand this migration as part of the normal ebb and flow of the contemporary church.

We are also able to team with the wider community. This past year two of the cluster churches worked with the Health Department of Durham Region and Sunrise Youth Services (an agency dedicated to special needs youth) to open a Friday night drop-in youth center for our community. By pooling our talents and resources, we multiply the ministry.

The paradigm of love

One of my favorite passages in scripture is Paul's first letter to the Corinthian church:

Love is patient, love is kind; love is not envious or boastful or arrogant or rude. It does not insist on its own way; it is not irritable or resentful; it does not rejoice in wrongdoing, but rejoices in the truth. It bears all things, believes all things, hopes all things, endures all things.[9]

We read this passage at weddings and apply it to married love. But we should also read it at covenanting services when new clergy are installed, or at the anniversary of the pastor's call. For this is what lies at the heart of our pastoral relationship. Each of us needs this type of love in our lives and in our relationships. I'm very clear that I love my people and my church, and I have told them so in worship. I believe that we should love our people with all our hearts, minds, and strength. Equally, the people who fill our pews are called to love each other with that same enthusiasm – including loving the minister!

This doesn't mean that we at Westminster are free of conflict or disagreement, or that I don't make mistakes. It has meant that we work together as a community, accepting and forgiving each other, with all our strengths and flaws. By being fully human and open, the ministry of the church flourishes.

A desert people

Richard LeSueur is my father's rector at St. Clement's Anglican Church in Toronto. While teaching in Jerusalem for five years, he learned about the Bedouin people. From them, he formulated rules for desert living that speak to clergy about to leave Elim and head into the wilderness.

1. *Never go into the desert alone,* because you can die so quickly. Clergy today are isolated and lonely. They need to have guides, mentors, and friends to share their burdens.

2. *Take only what you can carry.* Bring your flock, care for them, guide them to living water. You'll need a tent – a Bedouin tent where the sides roll up so there is room for the whole tribe, that community of care we depend upon for our sustenance. The tribe is always on the move, as is the church today. Decide what's important, and leave the rest behind.

3. *Expect anxiety.* The desert is a fearsome place and the way ahead is not clear. Leadership at any time is a fearful job; the admonition is "Be not afraid," not "Have no fear."

4. *Wait for God to speak in the burning bush.* In the desert, you have to wait. But know that the day of the Lord will come, the desert shall rejoice and blossom. Be patient, for "they that wait upon the Lord shall renew their strength."

Ways of leading

In seminary, I was told this parable as an illustration of leadership by facilitating:

A group of people was lost in the forest. While wandering through the woods, they came upon a holy person. "Ah," they said. "This person is wise and holy and can lead us out of the woods."

The holy person turned to the people and replied, "My children, I too am lost. But perhaps together we can find a way out of the woods."

It was a great story. But unfortunately, I was never told how it ended. I'm afraid it might be something like this:

One day, while still lost in the woods, one who had gone ahead came running back to the group. "A fire is coming towards us on one side," the scout cried, "and hungry wolves stalk us from the other. What are we to do?"

They went to the holy person and asked for leadership. But the holy person demurred. "Ah, my children," he said, "it is not up to me to tell you what to do. You must listen to yourselves."

So the people set up a series of working groups and study sessions on wolves and forest fires. They appointed chairpeople and struck committees. After much deliberation, they developed a draft document and sent it to their executive, who considered it and sent it back for further review.

The wolves had barbecue for lunch.

That's where we seem to be today – fires on one side, wolves on the other. What are we to do?

In a nutshell, lead. Lead an organism, not an organization. The old style of leadership, based on a top down, patriarchal model, won't work. We cannot command the feet to move forward. But neither can we simply facilitate discussions. Knees and eyes have to do more than just communicate with each other – they have to act together.

So we need to lead from the heart. To have the strength to share our vision, and the ability to adjust that vision to fit new circumstances. Leading today must be transparent and honest. It means being vulnerable, deeply human, and willing to admit when we are wrong.

The days are long past where leaders can impose their will on obedient flocks. But the alternative is not to huddle in the weeds hoping we won't offend anyone. Like Aaron and Moses we have to live with the murmurs, leave Elim, and get going through the wilderness – even if it takes us 40 years to get to a Promised Land that we may never see.

Names and Memories

DONNA SINCLAIR

> *Then Jacob asked him, "Please tell me your name."*
> *But [the stranger in the night] said, "Why is it that you ask*
> *my name?" And there he blessed him.*
> Genesis 32:29

> *To what shall I compare this generation? It is like children*
> *sitting in the marketplaces and calling to one another,*
> *"We played the flute for you, and you did not dance;*
> *We wailed and you did not mourn."*
> Matthew 11:16–17

I have seen it many times. The death of someone too young. A disease or a winter highway claims another victim, and the church sanctuary is filled, packed, with the stunned and grieving. In the choir, we wait to offer our words, sung like a lullaby that is entirely inadequate and entirely necessary, part of the ritual of mourning and remembering that the church offers.

"Wait," we sing to shattered faces that we dare not look at for fear we start to sob, "wait, there is more than this. Look," we sing, "God is welcoming your friend. No one is alone. If you do not believe this," we sing, "fear not. We will believe it for you."

I am a wavering and insufficient soprano. But I sometimes sense that this is one of the most important things I do.

The power of names

Singing those songs of confidence and hope when there is no hope is one reason why I trust that God will save the church. Perhaps not without great change – that's what this book is about. But God, having promised not to give up on the world again (God tried that once already; read the story of Noah), will always give the world what it needs – the flute with which to dance, the songs with which to mourn.

The world, like "children calling to each other in the marketplace," seldom knows this. So the church, now more than ever, runs foolishly, stubbornly, counter to the culture. That is both its vulnerability and its great strength. Because this contrariness is lived out in the congregation as much as anywhere, it is important for congregations to name and cherish the various forms this friendship with God takes.

A couple of hours drive north of where I live in northern Ontario is a community called Beaver House. A small group of very independent, unregistered Algonkian live on a lake about 30 kilometers from the mining town of Kirkland Lake. There is extensive moose pasture on the North Arm of the lake, so close to their community that even the old people can still hunt.[1]

It's lovely there. On a warm summer evening you can sit and watch the stars, fierce and bright in the absence of electricity.

One of the former chiefs, a gentle youngish woman named Emma MacPherson, whose ancestors set traps where the town of Kirkland Lake is now, has undertaken a massive project. She is preserving the Algonkian names for every river and inlet, every rock face, every hill in the area. She is determined these true names will not be obliterated by those who came hunting for gold at the turn of the 20th century.

Using a different language

This is the same job, in a way, that congregations do. They try to remember true names. Creation. The poor. The meek. The persecuted. The widows. The orphans. Those who hunger and thirst. The rich. Beloved. Child.

It's important that we know all these true names, because – as Emma MacPherson knows – the quality of our relationship with them depends upon it. Once those names are gone, the only names they have will be the ones given to them by others whose values are quite different. The first thing that missionaries did in Africa, the first thing some administrators did in our own residential schools for Native people, was to give the people new names. English names. Reflecting, therefore, English/Christian culture. The first thing that cults continue to do is give new converts new names, to absorb them into their new culture with a new identity.

Beaver House itself is really *Misemaquish*, MacPherson says, a much warmer term than "house." It means "the beaver nest where the family is." Using the traditional name for the moose pasture, for instance, may remind all that the land around that moose pasture should continue to be held in common, not divided up for cottages.

Retired University of Toronto physicist and Quaker Ursula Franklin argues that new names are being infiltrated into our consciousness by what she refers to as "an army of marketeers...who run the country for the benefit of the occupier."

The goal of the occupiers is privatization, which, in its most brutal terms, means to provide investment and profit opportunities in all those areas that people previously had set aside as common holdings – culture, health care, education, publishing, housing, nature, sports, prisons. Once dismantled, the "public sphere" can be more easily "occupied" – turned over to what I call the Empire of the Marketeers. These warlords will convert the ill-health and misery and basic needs of our neighbors into investment opportunities for the next round of global capitalism.[2]

This occupying power does not wear uniforms, says Franklin, but they can be identified by their language – language that converts real people and real experiences into abstract generalities. By avoiding their language, we refuse to be absorbed into their mindset. Instead of saying "users and providers of health care," for instance, we might offer the now distinctly old-fashioned terms "doctors and nurses and patients." Instead of "consumers of education" we might use "teachers and students," for those who make up our "friends, families, and communities."

It's possible that congregations, strengthened in this by the inherent subversion of scripture, can use an even older language of resistance to counteract the pressure sweeping the world towards people-as-units, movable and expendable, of consumption or labor. People may be prophets and healers, disciples, believers. Men and women. And above all, brothers and sisters. With individual names: Jim, Lakshmi, Abdul, Seiichi, Paulo, Doris, Monique...

Where the players of the market use words like competitiveness, efficiency, downsizing, and above all profit, congregations can use words like mercy, grace, and love. We cannot avoid these words when we read from the Bible, or when we sing our hymns. "Amazing grace," we sing, "how sweet the sound..."

It's hard to imagine anything more opposed to the dominant market culture of today.

These sound like small things, perhaps. But they are enormous. The church's insistence, a congregation's insistence, on seeing others as "brother" and "sister," on seeing the earth as God's Creation, keeps alive an idea that often seems frail and wounded.

Keeping an idea alive

As I write, my newspaper is full of stories about a government's deliberate sacrifice of the environment for profit; about impoverished people stuck again with welfare cuts; about civil wars and ethnic cleansing and refugees. The weight of all this harm-doing seems insurmountable. But we do not have to reverse it ourselves. All we have to do to keep alive the notion that this is wrong – like the churches in what used to be East Germany, on the far side of the Berlin Wall, keeping the notion of freedom alive until a barrier that seemed so permanent collapsed under the weight of a thousand small efforts.

Ursula Franklin recalls for us the beginnings of the Reformation. Triggered by a final revolt over the sale of indulgences, the seemingly universal authority of a church in desperate need of renewal cracked and crumbled.

What I derive from such events in history is that no authoritarian structure, no matter how powerful it may seem, is really impregnable – that it can in fact be brought down. Every opposing action, every skirmish, every critique helps to bring closer the time when the occupying army will be thrown out. Exactly when that time will come…and what form it will take, no one can predict. What we do know for certain is that social justice does not come from passivity or non-caring. Justice must be struggled for. That is what life is, or should be all about – striving for justice.[3]

Ontario's Bruce County has been struck, like many rural areas in North America, with the effects of a changed economy. Agribusiness, free trade, and government policies that mandate school board amalgamations and hospital closures dictate the disappearance of tiny communities. The 21st century is arriving in a swirl of pain. Sometimes the church is all that is left, and its members, too, wonder how small you can become and still be vital.

In the midst of this, the local Women's Institute is putting up signs.[4] At one crossroads, for example, where nothing remains but a little church (Centenary United) a new sign appears: "The Community of Centenary." The Rev. Linda Stemp says that "there is a little dedication ceremony every time a new sign goes up. And there are signs all over, in all of these places where there were once communities."

It is a small form of resistance. While the forces that occupy our society – what Ursula Franklin calls the Army of Marketeers – insist that the past does not matter and that community is expendable in the interests of efficiency, this little group of women says no. Like Emma MacPherson, they will keep their ancestors – and the values of tenderness and loyalty they honored – alive.

Acts of resistance

People who dare to keep small churches open do this too. (Not that every small church should stay open. As authors Roy Oswald and Robert Friedrich remind us, demographics sometimes dictate that a church must close.[5]) But at other times, a period of discernment may lead its members to see that this church, this congregation, this community of people, really is necessary. As schools are closed and children are bussed away, as their friendly bank teller is transformed into a instant banking machine, they refuse to submit to the-way-things-are-now. Perhaps this little group of people is needed, here, to resist. To continue to call things by their true names. To say, in the face of globalization, that this is a community, the community of Christ.

Emma MacPherson and the women of the Women's Institute know that memory is important. Christians have remembered Jesus' stories and commandments for almost 2,000 years. Love one another. Take care of the children. The kingdom of God is like a mustard seed, so small, and so filled with potential.

Even before that, we remember how people were sustained by stories of God's care for them. During the Babylonian exile, for example, Daniel safe in the lion's den, emerging to the embrace of King Darius and the decree that the God of Daniel "is the living God, enduring forever..."[6] Or the huddled Israelites, Jacob's descendants, fleeing from an enraged Egyptian army, passing unscathed through the waters...[7]

Memory, like language, is what an occupying force seeks to destroy. That is, again, why the church – that is, each congregation, large or small – is a precious countercultural force. It has a memory, carried in words and in symbols: this is the baptismal font carved by my grandfather, this is the hymn my parents sang, this is the altar cloth my grandmother stitched, this is the cross, the bread, the wine… The memory of what we believe is always there, ready to burst into the present and transform the future.

There are many ways that counter cultural memory lives itself out.

Staying together

It is countercultural, for example, *when congregations refuse to become splintered away from each other.* In Canada at least there is a trend towards decentralization and regionalism. Power is moved away from the center. In government this has led to endless constitutional debate and "devolution" of authority. In churches it manifests itself as congregationalism at the expense of national bodies – a yearning to be like the megachurches perhaps, that discard denominational labels to stand on their own.

There is nothing sacred about national offices. But what they safeguard *is* sacred: the connections between congregations, the sense of other members of denominations as brother and sister, the conviction that other Christians can help discern God's way for us.

As Oswald and Friedrich explain, it is the ability to test "our options with a community of faith" that enables us to distinguish "messages from God and messages from others." When we are desperate, it is only human to "see the easy way out as a message from God."

Not only do individual Christians need to be connected to a community, but communities of faith need to be connected with other congregations to establish a built-in source of guidance and correction.[8]

Note that they don't suggest the guidance and correction comes directly from national offices. Nobody has a lock on all the answers. But the denominational offices offer us a way to talk to one another that we might not otherwise have. If the church is "the body of Christ," then our national offices are the nerve centers that let one hand know what the other is doing.

As long as national offices exist as a clearinghouse, there is no need to keep re-inventing the wheel. When one small congregation finds something that works, others can know about it. When one congregation is in pain and conflict, others can help to mediate, or can offer possible solutions.

Above all, the church as a national or international body can do the overview and analysis – and thus offer the data – that one small congregation on its own could not. In my own city of North Bay, many years ago, the downtown center was threatened (as so many small city centers are) by a giant shopping mall to be built on the edge of town. The city councillors seemed enthusiastic about the project, despite the alarm of the merchants in the downtown core.

The inner-city congregation to which I belong got into the debate when it realized that seniors – many living downtown – would suffer if the area surrounding them decayed. Using models developed by our national church, several congregations got together and hired a researcher. Then they submitted data to city council showing the damage unlimited (and subsidized) growth on the outskirts of town would do.

It was one factor, perhaps a small one, in slowing down the pace of the development until the downtown merchants could regroup. The city continues to have a viable and even thriving downtown today.

It's a powerful argument for the continued presence of denominational bodies as treasure-houses of knowledge on widely varying topics. How to sponsor a refugee. How to oppose unhealthy development. Where to seek a theology in tune with the needs of the land. What retreat centers are available when we need peace to reflect on our lives.

And why the gospel might call us to do all of the above.

Staying faithful

It is countercultural *when a congregation trusts the logic of God instead of the logic of the world.*

The world's logic says – sometimes sadly, to be sure – that only the strong survive. Sometimes it turns harsher than that, and lies, saying that the poor are lazy, undeserving of anything better.

But some congregations trust the logic of God. They offer dignity to the impoverished. Oh, they often disguise it as a food bank – but with the coffee pot bubbling and interested volunteers telling jokes and an emphasis on the impoverished running the place themselves, it's really a loving community where the poor and the outcasts can find strength.

Some congregations offer a job network for those seeking employment. It's a lot of work, but it too offers ways for the impoverished to serve each other with renewed strength.

When politicians seek to scapegoat the poor, some congregations hold forums to try to tell the truth, or to do advocacy work in any number of vocal and persistent ways.

Many congregations haven't the resources to do these things, or they are too poor themselves, or their members are too tired, or logic of the world has blinded their eyes. That's all right. They can still follow God's logic by learning how to pray well, by listening to God, and opening themselves up to God's direction for their mission.

"Our real work is in the praying prior to our board work," say Oswald and Friedrich. The rest of the meeting flows out of that prayer.

What follows prayer is not so much a reasoned approach to things as a genuine listening to one another, being open to a solution to an issue that is not very rational but that instead just feels right to the entire group present… Our focus will not be on doing the rational, prudent thing, but rather on doing the faithful thing.[9]

Taking a different stance

It is countercultural *to be interior rather than exterior, soft rather than hard, mystical rather than practical.*

Each autumn for several years, a group of us from our congregation went to a nearby fishing lodge for a weekend. At an off-season rate, the proprietor served up bountiful camp meals suitable for a long day's fishing or, in our case, a long day's hard work honoring and interpreting our dreams. We kept a fire going all day and all night in a big cast-iron stove, and we talked to each other about matters of the soul that people seldom share.

Sometimes a few of us would walk in the bright autumn woods, or along the shore, thinking about what had been said. It was quiet and smoky and contemplative.

After a few years, we began meeting once a month at church as well. We gathered, ten or 20 or sometimes 30 people, to listen carefully to each other and carefully, cautiously, offer ideas about how a dream might be approached, what the symbols in it could mean. To support each other in an occupation most would find unusual – taking our dreams seriously.

People sometimes made life decisions, partly out of those gentle groups: to move, to stay, to take a risk, to be careful. They learned things about themselves. It wasn't always perfect. Mistakes were made. Sometimes people tried too hard to interpret someone else's dream. But mostly it involved listening at a very deep level and talking about matters of the heart.

It isn't the way we do things, in a fast-paced world. That's why it was church. I believe the future church will do more of this.

The wisdom of age

It is countercultural *to be old.*

Many of us in congregations are fearful about a preponderance of gray heads at Sunday worship. Perhaps we should worry less. Not only does worry lead to burnout, if overdone, but it also marks unthinking acceptance of a culture that idolizes youth.

Rather, we might make a deliberate effort to honor our elders. People in their 70s and 80s are just as alive and worthy as those in their 20s. In a time of transition like this one, caught between the church that knew clearly what it was called to do and the church that is yet to be born, our elders fulfill the function of some scholars and monks at another time – to keep memory alive. For there have been other times when the Christian church was just as lost as our own, times when it was struggling to keep learning alive in the Dark Ages, to find its way in the harsh environment of the late Middle Ages, for example. Editor, historian, and commentator Martin Marty describes how, despite the darkness

there were still bright comets that sped across the sky. There was still holiness in the lives of men and women who rose above the limits of their times… [They] could at the same time distinguish themselves for research and the routine copying of ancient manuscripts, and for cultivating a language of devotion with a simple but mystical bent that survives to our day.[10]

I'm not suggesting that our elders should busy themselves copying manuscripts. But in their persons, they often carry a tradition of loyalty and generosity to the church that seems antique in these days of institutional distrust. We need to mark that loyalty carefully. The time will come again when God will speak to us, offering a vision. And when that happens, we will need someone (as young Samuel needed old Eli, for example) who remembers how God's voice sounds.

Countercultural congregations

So what does all this mean for people in congregations right now? It means we should be alert both for the flute Jesus talks about in Matthew, and the wailing. Dancing and mourning are both signs of resistance in an unfeeling culture. They are small things. But as Ursula Franklin suggests, "Every critique helps to bring closer the time when the occupying army will be thrown out."

And we should not lose hope in our ability to run counter to the conquering culture of our times, and to affect it. In other countries, congregations have already done this on a more literal level than we normally see in North America.

The churches of East Germany in 1987, for example. They were filled with informers. Even Bible study was monitored, and rare visitors from the West were carefully scrutinized. In an officially atheistic country, adolescents who admitted to being Christian had trouble getting a place at university. Uniformed Soviet soldiers occupied the country. It was a cold harsh climate for the church and for anyone yearning for freedom. And there was no notion it would ever end. People were still being shot when they tried to cross the Berlin Wall. When I visited with a small group of church people that year, the parents in one of our host families were terribly worried that their son and daughter-in-law would be among those making the often-fatal attempt to start a new life in the West.

Yet just two years later, the shattered remnants of the hated wall were being pocketed for souvenirs by cheering crowds.

Nobody had any way of knowing for sure that this would happen. But it had – thanks to the stamina, the leadership, and the protests of people who, in many cases, had coalesced around the church.

North America has its own wall. It's rising between rich and poor, between the haves and the have-nots. The church that will live into the future is the one that names the wall for what it is – a sin, a terrible loss of freedom, a breaking of God's law – and fights unceasingly to bring it down.

Wherever any culture or society puts up walls, the church must keep chipping away at them. Jesus set us the model – what scholars such as John Dominic Crossan and Marcus Borg term a "radical egalitarian inclusivity." It was the mark of his ministry; he opened his arms, his heart, his teaching, to anyone willing to listen.

Jacob did a profoundly countercultural act, when he sought forgiveness and reconciliation with his brother. And Esau did the same, when he welcomed back the brother who had swindled him.

We carry these memories with us, to act upon, and treasure.

Encountering the Economy

CHRISTOPHER WHITE

Jacob said, "Please accept my gift that is brought to you,
because God has dealt graciously with me,
and because I have everything I want."
Genesis 33:11

Last summer I sat at a wedding reception between a bishop and a banker. (This is not the opening line of a terrible clergy joke.) As the evening progressed, I got into conversation with the banker. At one point, I asked him what concerned him about our current economy.

"The growing wage gap between the richest and the poorest members of our society," he said.

That was not the answer I was expecting from a banker.

"I have a real concern that when the next recession hits," he went on, "the full impact of government cutbacks will hit us and people will fall through the safety net, and that's when you can get social unrest."

I was stunned. This is the sort of answer that I would have expected from the bishop, sitting on my other side.

But the banker wasn't finished: "But you can't tell this to the people who are making huge bonuses and going out and purchasing a new Porsche. They don't see how that distorts the economy."

Experiencing an economic earthquake

Something is happening in the economy. In my own congregation I have lost track of how many people have lost their jobs in the seven years of my ministry. People who had one lifetime job in the 1980s are on their fourth or fifth in the late 1990s.

One great change in this past decade has been in the way employees are treated. People are disposable. They no longer receive loyalty from their employer. This has a corrosive effect upon the social fabric, as people become concerned primarily with survival – their own, and their family's. Loyalty and commitment to anything but the individual interest seems to be disappearing. Parts of the social safety net once deemed essential are now treated as luxuries we can no longer afford.

This is not only a North American condition. It is global. In *One World Ready or Not: The Manic Logic of Global Capitalism,* author William Greider documents the impact of globalization. In an interview, Rodney Jones of the Quantum Fund explained to Greider what happened to Thailand:

"Look at Thailand," said Quantum Funds' Rodney Jones. "They are raising the minimum wage, and that has decimated their textile sector. The production is moving to China, to Indonesia, to Vietnam. Something that started out as well-meaning is costing jobs. In five years Thailand won't have a textile sector."[1]

What is true for Thailand is equally true for Canada and the United States. When capital is free to travel, it will go to the lowest wage economies it can find.

Clive Allen is the executive vice president and chief legal officer for Nortel, formerly Northern Telecom, one of Canada's most successful high-tech companies. In a speech he gave in Cleveland, Allen made the following point:

Northern and other companies on the list of Canadian players owe no allegiance to Canada. Just because we (Nortel) were born there doesn't mean we'll remain there. Canadians shouldn't feel that they own us.[2]

As *Toronto Star* columnist Richard Gwyn commented, in the eyes of global corporations there is no loyalty of any kind anymore.

What made this string of comments so insightful was the way Allen took for granted not just that corporations like his in fact owe no allegiance to their country, but that they should owe no allegiance.

One month after Allen's speech in Cleveland, Nortel announced that it was closing three Canadian plants and laying off 2400 workers.

North Americans have for years assumed that corporations had their best interests in mind. The old saying, "What's good for GM is good for the United States," had some truth to it. GM made profits, and the workers of the United States and Canada got good jobs, good wages, good benefits, and lifetime employment. The postwar world for North America was, in a real sense, a golden age – for industry as it was for congregations.

While we in North America benefited hugely from the postwar boom, that time is now history. We are now truly a global economy. And as New Zealand financier Rodney Jones bluntly put it: "Where is it written that white guys in Britain are entitled to $15 an hour and five weeks holiday while Asians are supposed to work for $3.00 a day?"[3]

The causes of the crisis

Global corporations, it is now clear, serve their own needs first. Any benefits to the workers or the host nations are unintended by-products.

There are two major theories for how this change came about. The first, supported by writers, such as Jeremy Rifkin, holds that computer technology has changed all the economic rules. Computerization smashed the link between labor and productivity.

While earlier industrial technologies replaced the physical power of human labor, substituting machines for body and brawn, the new computer-based technologies promise a replacement of the human mind itself, substituting thinking machines for human beings across the entire gamut of economic activity. In the United States alone, that means in the years ahead more than 90 million jobs in a labor force of 124 million are potentially vulnerable.[4]

All of us have been affected by the impact of this new technology. The computer on which I am writing this chapter can perform tasks that my father could only dream of when he was writing his books in the 1960s and 1970s. Rifkin links the impact of computerization at the work place to the increase in part-time work, the decline of the nation state, and the end of blue collar labor.

But not all agree with Rifkin.

Business writers William Wolman and Anne Colamosca blame not technology but capital for the present situation. In their book *The Judas Economy,* they rebut Rifkin's thesis:

Dire warnings about the impact of technology on labor as a whole have been common throughout history and have always proved wrong. The jobs lost in declining industries or among workers using obsolete technologies have always been replaced by new jobs in new industries using new technologies.[5]

Instead, they believe that the problem is the triumph of capital. The ability of capital to cross borders and migrate to low wage economies is what causes such pain and dislocation.

This concept is shared by George Soros, a billionaire financier who has built a personal and corporate fortune through his understanding of financial markets. In *The Crisis of Global Capitalism,* Soros claims that our current addiction to letting markets control our economies is leading us into very dangerous waters. He calls it "market fundamentalism" – a system of economic beliefs accepted as blindly as religious fundamentalism.

It is market fundamentalism that has rendered the global capitalist system unsound and unsustainable… Market fundamentalism is today a greater threat to open society then any totalitarian ideologies… Market forces, if they are given complete authority, even in purely economic and financial areas, produce chaos and could ultimately lead to the downfall of the global capitalist system.[6]

He too sounds more like a bishop than a banker.

The church is not an island

No matter where you live or what your job, the combination of the free flow of capital across national borders and rapidly changing technology keeps us in a constant state of dis-ease and uncertainty. As Wolman and Colamosca write:

Bangalore [India] has quietly put together all the ingredients of a broad frontal attack on American hegemony on the frontier of the information revolution, software. India's software industry, which barely existed 10 years ago, has been growing 40% a year…It currently costs about one third as much in India to do what is done in the United States – even with the thousands of miles of distance.[7]

Two kinds of economies

Yet are we not in the midst of the greatest boom in postwar history? In North America the stock market daily seems to reach new heights. Unemployment is quite low in the United States and appears to be dropping in Canada. So what on earth can be wrong?

Economist Jim Stanford explains the dichotomy of our current economic situation in his book *Paper Boom*. He divides the economy into two sectors, the paper economy of the financial institutions and the "real" economy that affects the rest of us:

The financial economy (also called the paper economy) represents the huge industry that has developed around the creation, purchase, and sale of money and other financial (paper) assets: stocks, bonds, loans, mortgages, mutual funds, derivatives, foreign currency, annuities... Yet despite the apparent importance of finances, in a fundamental sense its operations are tangential to the economic life of a country. This is because the activity of the financial sector – its "output" – does not directly contribute to the material well-being or productivity of Canadians. It is the real economy that produces the products and services that contribute concretely to our material standard of living.[8]

For Stanford, the "real" economy deals in those elements that we actually consume and use. Food, clothing, transportation, entertainment. Also, products and services that governments and public institutions generate, such as health care, schools, road construction, plus the raw materials, spare parts, and machinery used by Canadian business.

Unfortunately for us, it's the paper economy that's booming. Less then 5 percent of the paid workforce has benefited from it. The remaining 95 percent, employed in the "real" economy, has struggled and seen incomes decline. In the 1990s the real unemployment rate (including those who have given up looking for work) has topped 12 percent. Combined with poor job creation, much of it part-time, this has led to our current malaise.

Stanford believes that we need to invest heavily in the real economy, create alternate credit options for business, and limit the international movement of capital. He would do that through the use of the so-called "Tobin Tax," which would collect a small tax on cross border financial transactions to discourage speculation and add badly needed stability to our current system of finance.[9]

This disparity between the two economies does much to explain our current situation. Why, on the one hand, the waiting list for a new Mercedes can be a year; on the other, my neighbor hasn't had a raise in over eight years! A minority are enjoying a boom, while the majority are, in the words of the correspondent I quoted in **Blessing 8,** "hanging on by their fingernails, hoping the whole house of cards won't collapse before they can retire or get the hell out."

Stewardship

If the present state of world economics affects our lives, and affects our incomes, it affects the church. The church is not an island. We may profess that our Kingdom is not of the world, but we are certainly in it. These seismic changes have implications for stewardship, for pastoral care, and for programming.

The stewardship issue is clearest. If incomes continue to decline, how can we fund our churches?

The very word "stewardship" brings forth uncomfortable feelings and nervous glances around most churches. Stewardship is to congregations as a root canal is to dental care. A few congregations have had regular stewardship programs every year for 20 years. But in most churches, mentioning "stewardship" gives members of the congregation that sinking feeling that their wallets are about to get hurt. And they don't welcome it. Every day, they're deluged with donation requests from worthy charities; their mailboxes are full of bills; and their paycheques seem to deduct as much in taxes and benefits as they get to take home. They hope that the church will be a refuge from all that, and then, wham! they get hit with the pitch to dig deeper.

Clergy have an additional reason for that sinking feeling – conflict. As soon as a stewardship campaign gets announced, they want to barricade their offices, rip out their phones, and avoid any casual conversations. For they know that someone will get offended by the stewardship campaign and walk out, never to return to the church again. Others will complain – sometimes vociferously – and they'll expect the clergy to fix it.

Wishing for a magic wand

If I had a magic wand, I would wave it and make all the stresses and pain associated with stewardship disappear, and in their place create a wonderful experience of deepening faith and commitment. But I can't do that. I don't have a magic wand. I don't even believe in magic wands. I live and work in a real congregation filled with real people, struggling with real lives, trying to honor all their commitments without being overwhelmed.

Instead, let me tell you a story – a real story, the story of our stewardship campaign at Westminster United Church in Whitby, Ontario.

Over a year ago, at a well attended congregational meeting, Westminster voted to add a part-time parish nurse to our staff. I described the results of that decision in **Blessing 4, The Whole Person**. The question came, "How are we going to pay for this?" We decided to hold a stewardship campaign that spring.

First, we embarked on an interview process for consultants. That alone was an eye opener. Most of them were not concerned so much about stewardship as they were about fund raising. The majority of them were theologically very conservative. And they worked for a substantial fee, plus a percentage of the funds raised. We only found one consultant who reflected mainstream theology and whose charges were, in our view, fair and reasonable.

We soon realized a number of things. First, that this was going to be more work than we had bargained for. Second, it wasn't about money. Money may have been "the presenting issue," as therapists like to say. But the central concern was commitment. According to our consultants, donations in my denomination are among the lowest in North American churches. Our congregation's were among the lowest of the low.

Without knowing it, we had unintentionally created a thriving, very busy, low-commitment church. You wouldn't know it on a Sunday, because the place is packed. We had to hold two services to cope with our numbers, and our Sunday school topped 200, all in a relatively small building.

We had been the welcoming church, the friendly church. Now we were faced with changing the ethos of our congregation into a high-commitment church in a matter of months.

As we continued to plan, we quickly realized that there was no way that our spring target was going to be met. We postponed it to the fall. That was the right decision, but it had its consequences. Stewardship campaigns in the spring benefit from income tax refund time. Extra money is coming back, people's moods are brightened by the warmer weather, and it's a good way to finish the program year before the summer doldrums.

By moving the campaign to the fall we came up against what I call the "fall shellout." Every organization is starting up, and every organization wants money. In our house it's school, ballet, and skating. As well, early September is church-shopping month for potential new members. Walking in to discover that a church is embarking upon a multiple-month stewardship campaign had visitors stampeding towards the exits. For the past seven years we had had significant increases in attendance every fall. Our stewardship campaign solved that problem overnight.

Changing the ethos of a church

But we persevered. We organized faith discussion groups and scheduled speakers for Sunday morning faith sharing. We planned the congregational meals, worked on the narrative budget, edited the stewardship information package, and argued over the every member visitation. The more we worked, the greater our commitment.

Then we launched the project.

After the first Sunday's presentation, I had one letter of resignation. Several others were deeply annoyed. A few people thought it was wonderful. Those diverse reactions set the tone for the next eight weeks. People hated the faith sharing during worship; people loved the faith sharing during worship. People hated the faith discussion groups; people loved the faith discussion groups. People hated the meals; people loved the meals. Some thought the narrative budget (expressing our goals in words instead of just in figures) was wonderful and clear; others thought it was muddy and confusing. Some people welcomed being asked to make an annual pledge of time, talents, and treasure; others considered the whole pledging process an unwarranted intrusion into their personal lives. Opinions ranged from those who thought the whole project was valuable and worthwhile, to those who thought the whole thing a colossal waste of time.

It was the single most difficult experience I've had in the church in the last decade.

But when the pledge forms came in, givings immediately went up over 20 percent. Four months later, that had increased to 27 percent. We ended last year with a surplus rather than a deficit.

By any measure, the campaign was a resounding success. We changed the culture of the church, we weathered the storms, and I survived. We are now a pledging, committed congregation. It was hard, at times it hurt, but I believe that every church needs to do this.

Meeting needs requires money

To survive into the future, the mainline church will have to turn itself into a collection of high-commitment congregations. To be blunt, the church needs to have first call upon the charitable contributions and time of its members.

Loren Mead, in *Financial Meltdown in the Mainline,* says so too. Because, he says, there are a number of fiscal "unexploded bombs"[10] just waiting to blow up under an unsuspecting church. Those bombs include municipalities looking for ways of assessing property taxes on church buildings. And governments taxing clergy deductions for housing allowances. Allowable charitable deductions being reduced. Churches being sued for abuse suffered half a century ago. On top of all that, misappropriation and embezzlement of funds by some senior church officials have destroyed confidence. All of these will have significant consequences upon our finances.

Without congregations committed to the church, we cannot meet the ministry needs of our communities or pay our bills. Especially during fiscally conservative times, when governments continually cut back on social services, the church is desperately needed as a living force in our community, reaching out to the marginalized from a strong basis of faith and resources.

So we need to change our culture. The good news is that it can be done. Westminster did it, and so can you

If our focus is outward we will thrive. All around us people are experiencing a breakdown in community. Francis Fukuyama makes it clear in an article in the *Atlantic Monthly,* titled "The Great Disruption." Community has been lost, he says, and religion will have to have a central role if it is to be recovered:

People will return to religion not necessarily because they accept the truth of revelation, but precisely because the absence of community and the transience of social ties in the secular world makes them hungry for ritual and cultural tradition. They will help the poor or their neighbors not necessarily because doctrine tells them they must but rather because they want to serve their communities.[11]

But it is clear to me that if we simply look internally, we will wither away. God will find others to do God's work.

This is the point that Robert Wuthnow makes in his sobering book, *The Crisis in the Churches: Spiritual Malaise, Financial Woe.* Wuthnow believes that the church, its pastors, and its congregations have lost the link between faith and economic activity. Stewardship has disappeared, and the church is in danger of disappearing with it.

Many church members say that they are tired of hearing the clergy beg for money... But most church members do want their church to be more supportive to working families, to speak against materialism, and to draw practical applications for their lives. The opportunity is thus present for churches to minister to the economic concerns of their parishioners.[12]

An alternative kind of community

Wuthnow also argues that the churches' failure to articulate the linkage between work, money, and faith has deepened our current crisis. He believes that we desperately need to recover stewardship, which for him includes a commitment to social justice.

Despite the current obsession with "big box" megachurches, Wuthnow puts his hope in the mid-sized church (which in the U.S. would be 200–500 members, and about half that size in Canada). On a scale of sizes, from rural or family churches to megachurches, he calls these "program churches."

The program church is small enough to foster community among its members, to enlist volunteer help, and to give its clergy a prominent voice within the congregation, but not so small that it must worry about keeping its doors open at all. The program church…can create a distinct niche for itself as a place where people are especially challenged to work for social justice, to become involved in serving the needy, or to give sacrificially to missions and evangelism projects.[13]

These views all emphasize the same point, in different ways. The church is an alternate community, one of the last on the planet. We don't put advertising on our pews. My preaching stole bears a cross, not a Nike Swoosh. I saw a report, somewhere, that McDonald's "Golden Arches" is now the best known symbol in the world. When corporate advertising permeates even the computer screens and classrooms of our children's schools, when people pay extra so that they can promote someone's product on their T-shirts, when arts and culture cannot survive without the sponsorship of a tobacco company or a brewery, we in the church represent something different and vital. In the Middle Ages, the church was the repository of learning and health. In this age, churches may be the repository of sanity.

Two members of my congregation recently lost their jobs. While the out-placement service helped one of them, the other felt very much alone and isolated. They found tremendous support in simply talking to each other. Together, they discussed the sense of dislocation, the shock of being let go, the uncertainty and embarrassment they felt. They were able to bolster one another as they went on their job interviews. They found a community in their shared experience.

Part of our role is to provide opportunities for people hurt by today's economic earthquake to meet and share experiences. To share information on how to survive the change, and advice on finding new meaning in their lives. Churches have done this before during recessions, but I suspect that now it needs to be a permanent feature of our landscape.

In addition, churches need financial resources that can be allocated as transition funds to help families in crisis due to layoffs or plant closings. With the extraordinarily high levels of personal debt that North Americans carry, many are only a paycheque away from catastrophe.

Making a difference

But while the church can provide support and encouragement, we can do more. We must, in my view, become active economic players. Churches have huge financial resources under their roofs. At one small congregation, the members balked at increasing the church's annual budget. "We don't have that much money," they protested.

The campaign manager looked around and did a quick mental calculation. "The people sitting in this sanctuary have over $2 million a year to spend," he replied. "The only question is what we choose to spend it on."

Imagine the purchasing power of hundreds of thousands of Christians throughout our continent. Imagine the potential of harnessing that for the benefit of our communities.

For example, in Canada we have Registered Retirement Savings Plans that help us save for our retirement years. Millions of dollars are poured into them annually. Imagine the impact if we all invested in the so-called Ethical Funds – most of which won't invest in tobacco, alcohol, or weapons. Other Mutual Fund companies would have to offer similar funds to compete; companies would vie to be on the approved list. The economic landscape would change – for the better, in my opinion. And based on the recent history of Ethical Funds we would all do quite well financially, too.

Gordon Powers, who writes a mutual fund column for *The Globe and Mail,* one of Canada's national newspapers, points out that in the United States there are already a wide variety of socially responsible investment options. In Canada, we have a way to go. But he believes that investments more clearly screened for ethical behavior can affect corporate behavior; he calls ethical investments the wave of the future.[14]

Alternatively, Jim Standford suggests,[15] we could take as little as 2 percent of what we invest and donate that to projects on economic development or social change. That could include projects of our national denominations.

Whatever we choose to do, our investments can affect people's lives for the better.

An entrepreneurial vision

Some of you may conclude from my analysis of our global economy that I am an old style socialist! Far from it. I believe in business. I believe in the power of investment to bring about change. I support small and medium enterprises. After all, my spiritual ancestor Jacob profited rather nicely from his genetic experiments with his brother-in-law Laban's herds. Jacob arrived in Laban's land with nothing; he left wealthy, with camels, livestock, wives, children, and a retinue of servants.

What I object to is the unbridled power of huge corporations to squash competition and override any interests other than their own. Like George Soros, I believe that an economy should serve the needs of people, not the other way round.

Soros believes that the missing element in our current economic model is the moral dimension.

If I had to deal with people instead of markets, I could not avoid moral choices…
Anonymous market participants are largely exempt from moral choices as long as they
play by the rules. In this sense, financial markets are not immoral, they are amoral.[16]

What I call "monopoly capitalism" is actually opposed to economic growth.
It thrives on destroying competition, not encouraging it. The economic and
social results of this were evident back in the 1950s. Walter Goldschmidt, a
researcher for the U.S. Department of Agriculture, studied two similar farm
communities in southern California. The economy in the community of
Dinuba was based on many small farms; in Arvin it depended on agribusiness.
As a community, Dinuba had higher median incomes and living standards. In
addition, the people of Dinuba had a higher quality of life. Schools and parks
were more numerous. The streets, waste treatment, and garbage facilities were
all superior to those of the agribusiness town.[17] Goldschmidt's study showed
that small truly was beautiful. Main Street is economically better for us then
Wall Street in New York, or Bay Street in Toronto.

The United States Department of Agriculture suppressed his report for
30 years because his report challenged economic orthodoxy – what economist John Kenneth Galbraith used to call "the conventional wisdom."

People don't like having their unquestioned assumptions questioned.
Just ask Bill Phipps, Moderator of The United Church of Canada. When he
set up an Internet discussion site on "The Moral Economy," he was savaged
by Andrew Coyne, a columnist for Canada's *National Post*.

Phipps actually considers this reaction a positive development. "It shows
I struck a nerve," he told me. He also believes that his Internet discussion
forum shows how the technology we create can be used to create communities of resistance, as well as to bluster us into submission. The withdrawal –
for the time being at least – of the Multilateral Agreement on Investment is
an example, he says, of grassroots people using the Internet to derail an
agreement that would have given global corporations the legal right to over-
rule national policies.

Showing the world what it's not doing

Yet the reaction to Phipps' initiative is nothing new to the church.

Ian Manson, a minister in Manitoba, did his doctoral thesis on his denomination's actions during the Great Depression of the 1930s. The Board of Evangelism and Social Service of the United Church of Canada developed a document called *Christianizing the Social Order*. Its pages contained a blueprint for what became known as the welfare state. As a response to the decade's economic calamity, it recommended unemployment insurance, government pensions, and medical care for all citizens (rights now taken for granted in Canada). Then as now, the church was vehemently attacked for meddling in places where it supposedly had no business.

The other role played by the church was in providing relief for the suffering. The National Relief Commission collected food, clothing, and other goods. These were shipped in hundreds and hundreds of rail cars to the west, where drought meant no crops, no clothing, and no food.

Once again, this parallels the churches' support for "Out of the Cold" programs, food banks, refugee sponsorships, and other relief programs for the poor and marginalized.

We should not expect society to be grateful when the church shows them that the emperor has no clothes. It is our task to act in love. By doing what we must, by doing what we believe Christ would do in our circumstances, we show the world what it is *not* doing. Thus we pay the price of being countercultural.

It is a price worth paying, for in spite of criticism and outright hostility, we do get results. The ecumenical Jubilee 2000 project has brought churches together from around the globe, dedicated to forgiving the crippling debts borne by the nations of the Two-Thirds World. Politicians and governments have been lobbied locally, nationally, and internationally. Petitions and education projects have raised the issue throughout the world. For the first time in human history, the G8 nations have agreed, in part, to reduce the burden of these debts. Without the work of the churches this would not have happened.

We are still an effective and vital force for good in the world. We should hold our heads up high. We *do* make a difference.

Expanding power through partnerships

Yet there is more to do. I hope that we will look to our partner churches in the Two-Thirds World for leadership. Especially in areas of economic development.

In 1986 I served as an overseas intern in Sierra Leone, West Africa. I remember Mustapha. Mustapha had polio. He worked out of his wheelchair. He was remarkable, not by the way he merely coped with a disability, but the way he prevailed over it. Like a modern Jacob, Mustapha began a blacksmith shop, which he then turned into a training facility for other young men who had also suffered polio. Through his energy and determination, they learn a skilled trade that gives them the means to build their own small businesses.

Mustapha also started a small rice and cassava farm to help feed his growing community. He even added a residence so people from all over Sierra Leone could visit and learn. It was an amazing place. Everything and everyone worked. There were no rusted out tractors in his project, no international aid funds misused or diverted to personal gain. Instead, his workshop arose out of community needs, used appropriate technology, and was a living symbol of hope in a land that many wrote off as hopeless.

When I returned to Canada, that project stuck with me in both my mind and heart. And when I moved back to Ontario in 1992 to discover my home province in the teeth of the worst recession since the 1930s, it was to Mustapha and the people of Sierra Leone that I turned for inspiration.

Out of this came a wonderful program and partnership. The church, Durham College (a community college known for its innovation and commitment to excellence), the Federal Business Development Bank, and Employment Canada created together a self-employment program for people on unemployment insurance and social assistance. Durham College housed the project, the FBDB supplied the teachers, and the church provided emotional and post-graduation support. The federal government funded the participants.

For two years, people picked up entrepreneurial skills that not only helped them in their own businesses, but made them more attractive to employers. We created everything from a mobile word processing firm, to retail stores, to one entrepreneur who specialized in children's hats. The business fairs we held showed the remarkable diversity of the people involved and modeled the hope that everyone so badly needed.

A footnote: as part of their recent belt-tightening process, the federal government cut our project's funding.

Despite that negative outcome, I learned a great deal from our self-employment project. I discovered that churches can make a difference. We are not alone; we can form partnerships with other people of good will to create hope and jobs. We can go beyond the Band-Aid relief of food banks.

I learned that we must act quickly, before unemployment saps self esteem and drains away energy and enthusiasm.

But I also learned that the economic system is not yet flexible enough to recognize the needs of fast growing micro-businesses. Banks, despite all their protestations of supporting small business, are not willing to risk their capital on unproven ventures. As churches, we need to provide working capital for this emerging sector. So, what if we, as churches, created credit unions, with mandates to invest in small enterprises and cooperatives? What if we harnessed all that potential that goes to the banks under our own roofs and sent it out into the economy?

Community-level economic development

It is, thank God, already happening. In *From Corporate Greed to Common Good,* Murray MacAdam documents the Canadian churches' involvement in community economic development projects. The Edmonton Recycling Society employs 82 people and contracts with the city of Edmonton to run part of the municipal recycling program. The Montreal Community Loan Association finances low-income entrepreneurs. These and other stories show how the church provides an alternate economic community.

Community economic development functions on four fundamental beliefs:[18]

* *Social and economic goals can and should be combined.* It's possible to develop businesses which are successful and which meet unfulfilled needs in society, such as environmental protection.
* *"Business as usual" just isn't good enough.* The mainstream economy still leaves many people on the sidelines, relegated to poverty, unemployment, and frustration.
* *Humans have a need to work;* good working and good living go together. Without work people lack pride, dignity, and a sense of worth.
* *Development is based on and affirms the role of community.* The community can be a community of interest, of geography, or of different types of people linked by willingness to work together for the common good.

These principles are working in the economy even now, but we have only scratched the surface of our potential.

Operation 2000, based in the twin cities of Kitchener-Waterloo in Ontario, aims to help 2,000 families move out of poverty by December 31, 2000, producing in those cities the lowest poverty rate in Canada. The story is on the Internet, at www.op2000.org. A unique partnership of church, business, government, and non-governmental agencies, it is developing everything from small business incubators to marketing co-ops, from a market garden to an artists' cooperative. As I write this, it has already created 5,800 new jobs, 1,000 new businesses, and 3,000 skills training or education upgrading opportunities. By the time you read this, those numbers will have increased.

The Operation 2000 model could be copied all over North America. The only thing stopping us is the unwillingness of churches in every community to became involved in like-minded projects. Not only could we increase economic self-sufficiency, but the church could actually help to create economic prosperity.

What better way to answer the growing gap between rich and poor on our continent?

Evangelism with Empathy

DONNA SINCLAIR

[Jacob said] "...for truly to see your face
is like seeing the face of God –
since you have received me with such favor."
Genesis 33:10b

By the rivers of Babylon,
there we sat down and there we wept
when we remembered Zion.
On the willows there we hung up our harps...
How could we sing the Lord's song in a foreign land?
Psalm 137:1–2, 4

When a friend of mine was growing up, her family were Jehovah's Witnesses. That meant she went as a child from door to door, witnessing about Jesus. Have you been saved? Do you know the Lord? Can I tell you about Jesus?

Her story frightens me. I wonder what was it like to stand at someone's door and knock, knowing you might be laughed at, knowing this might well be a household where no-one would listen – but understanding that this is what you were called to do by your faith? Sometimes people would send their dogs after her. Could I knock on a door, knowing I might be attacked?

What if God asked me to do that?

I firmly believe that God does expect me to evangelize, to share the Good News that I have experienced in Jesus Christ. But not by knocking on doors. Not by simply telling people turn to Jesus to be saved. And not just because I'm afraid of fierce dogs.

The insight came through other friends – some Jewish, some Native. I saw their commitment to their faith. For them, it was not something that they had to parade, that they had to persuade others to follow – it was something they lived, day in, day out. A Jewish friend and fellow-teacher calmly handed me her mixing bowl after I had used it to whip cream (she reserved it for meat); "It's yours now," she said. There was no hint of complaint or recrimination in her comment. She forgave me instantly for never taking the trouble to figure out the food laws of her people, even though I was her friend.

Native friends reach out to me past their memories of residential schools. They too forgive me, though I live inside the Christian institution that had hurt them.

It would be absurd, in the face of their persistent love, to say to them, "Give all this up. Turn to *my* faith, I insist, for I know The Only Way."

Singing the song

Still, like all Christians, I do have the Jesus-song. Even if I sometimes sing it badly, it gives me life. Others might want to sing it, too, if they knew it, because it brings us life beyond the words and music of consumerism. As theologian Walter Brueggemann writes, compared to the gospel, the inadequacies of those other songs we all carry are clear:

The stories [from our culture] we have embraced without great intentionality are not adequate. They…cannot generate the life for which we yearn… They lack the life-giving power of holiness out beyond our selves to which we must have access if we are to have fully human lives.[1]

But how are to we to sing of "holiness out beyond our selves" as Christians? After Auschwitz, after my people took Native children from their mothers and fathers and language, after Muslims were bombed in Iraq and members of Christian churches failed to pour into the streets in outrage?

The end of Christendom

In 1998, in a terrible tragedy just off Peggy's Cove in Nova Scotia, a Swissair flight on its way to Geneva from New York crashed into the icy water of the Atlantic Ocean. No one survived the crash; 229 people were killed.

Local people, including church members, sprang into action. They searched first for survivors and then, when there were none, for bodies. They appeared at emergency centers offering food, flowers, pastoral care. In the midst of anguish, humanity itself shone with sustained compassion. Day after day, people became living examples of Jesus' command to love one another.

Finally there was a memorial service at the Cove, with various representatives of many faiths taking part. And through some awkwardness in communication, Christian participants understood that they were to refrain from mentioning Jesus.

That instruction drives home a message. If you hadn't noticed it yet, we no longer live in Christendom – a society where it is universally accepted that any public ceremony will, at root, be Christian. Given the horrors through the ages that people calling themselves Christian have either allowed or fostered – think of the Crusades, the Inquisition, the witch-hunts of Salem – perhaps the disentanglement of faith from the status quo is, in Shakespeare's phrase, an outcome "devoutly to be wished."

But now that we are in exile, what does it mean to sing the Lord's song?

How are we to evangelize in the unknown land that is (as Loren Mead points out) right outside our church doors?[2] We can provide kitchens for those who are hungry for food, but what of those who long for Good News in the darkness of a sleepless night? What does our "mission" and our "evangelism" look like today?

Bringing people closer together

One clue is found in the outpouring of tenderness around that Swissair disaster. Long before the memorial service, local people had already found one superb form of mission. Christian ministers went to the disaster scene and quietly offered their skills in pastoral care. Fishing people, Christian and non-Christian alike, put their living bodies between the dark water and the grieving relatives, searching.

Cuban theologian Rene Castellanos defines evangelism as "whatever brings people closer together." Certainly, something was happening in that horrible disaster that brought people very close.

Castellanos' wisdom is born out of being Christian, and singing the Jesus song, in an officially Communist country. So he has already lived for many years in what is, for North American Christians, a strange land. But it is no stranger than the one we now inhabit ourselves, in which the Christian discipline of compassion inevitably places us at odds with the prevailing culture.

A questioner once asked Castellanos, "What is it like, trying to be a Christian in a Communist country?"

He replied gently, "What is it like, trying to be a Christian in a capitalist country?"

Learning to pay attention

Some of our own elders in the faith learned how to sing their song in a strange land. Perhaps their skills are needed now.

Katherine Hockin, for example, was a missionary in China until the Communists took over. I interviewed her a few years before her death, for a book about the Woman's Missionary Society which she had served. Hockin had thought a great deal about mission. For nine months, from December 1950 to November 1951, she was unable to secure an exit visa to return to Canada. She was both forbidden to work and forbidden to leave.

In that situation, Hockin listened hard:

My best Chinese friend came to me and said, "You must ask to go. You are not helpful." They had her come because we were closest and it must have been hard for her. It was hard for me to hear. From that time on I read what was being prepared for the Chinese church, their political study, and really listened.[3]

Her situation in China parallels ours in North America. When we look around, we observe that few people understand what we are about. Some (when churches call them to account over economic policy) may become actively hostile.

Hockin tried to understand the historical roots of what was happening in China. It wasn't easy. For one thing, she came down with typhoid. It was a time when the Chinese media were filled with talk of "germ warfare, and I was scared stiff that someone else around would get sick and blame me. Still, somehow, the people in the church heard I was ill and – [although] Aureomycin was not in great supply – they got enough to make me better."

And she kept on learning, despite a loudspeaker right beneath her window blaring anti-Western propaganda all day.

The thing that kept me at least sane and involved was reading the Chinese materials, the course (in Communist theory) that was being prepared. (I remember the foreign office would come and check on us, that we weren't putting poison in wells.) I thought it was important to understand.

The new generation of students – the older students were kept more distant – but the younger generation of students were very well indoctrinated and so whenever we got out they would say, "You are thieves. You are robbers. Everything you have belongs to China."

By the time Hockin finally returned to Canada, she had listened so carefully she understood the Chinese point of view:

I remember the day that I suddenly realized that if I was Chinese, I would hate me too, and that sort of gave me a new direction. I think it was the sense that this was an awfully important learning that brought me home and made me plead with church to be different. You just sit in a different position. It makes you very humble and I think you are a little more distant from certainty.

In other words you have to say, "What is God saying to us in this?"

Whatever our evangelism is to be today, it has to be humble. It will be extremely difficult for us to sing the Good News if our listeners interpret it as arrogance. It is difficult to share ministry with people when we feel we have the only way to salvation. That we have answers, instead of questions. That we offer solutions without sympathy.

Evangelism today runs both ways. That is risky. Many will fear that in humbly reaching out, in listening respectfully to others, we might forget who we are.

Doing the work

But the evangelism of today requires that kind of courage. We cannot evangelize from within the walls of a fortress; we have to be out there among the people, risking and vulnerable.

It is the kind of bravery Victoria Cheung displayed. I didn't interview her, even though, like Hockin, she was also a missionary who figured largely in the WMS. She was long dead by the time I got around to writing that story. But I found her letters in our national church's archives, and loved her artist's eye for detail:

The Easter lilies only started to bloom two weeks ago, but they were beautiful, and our friends brought pots, begging for them, promising to return the bulbs. I have two calla lilies today, the first growth of its kind here. The R.C. sisters gave me the slips they got from Manila last year, they also gave me 20 leghorn eggs, we hatched 14, they are most difficult beggars to raise. Our piggies are good and round, the ducks are lengthening out, the chickens are still fluffy and pretty while the kittens are becoming quite useful as well as ornamental, for there are plenty of mice around… And I've left out the wee gold fish, there are hundreds of them, just large enough to be noticeable, shimmering in the earthenware jar, nibbling sieved egg yolk. [4]

Trained in medicine by the WMS, Cheung had been sent to Kong Moon, China, in 1923, to work in the mission hospital there. Hidden by her Chinese ancestry, she managed, unlike Hockin, to remain in China through occupation and revolution.

In 1942, the worried treasurer of the South China Mission, T. A. Broadfoot, tried to get money to her. Cheung quickly wrote back: "I am in a dangerous position, and the Japanese would make it very difficult for me and my friends… Send no funds or salary."

But she had to leave her beloved hospital. As Broadfoot wrote in a report:

She was not allowed to continue living in the Mission Compound… Dr. Cheung, her mother, Dr. Wong [Cheung's assistant] and the two Chinese nurses worked long and laborious hours, walking miles in all kinds of weather, sacrificing themselves and in great danger. They secured a shop in the city of Kong Moon and built up a very successful clinic, where much valuable medical and hospital work is now carried on. [5]

Cheung could not openly sing the song of Jesus; but she was clearly doing his time-honored work of healing, even though remaining in China to do so ultimately required her to sever her ties with her church. A final, poignant note in her file was added by an unknown hand:

All Dr. Cheung's service was in the hospital at Kong Moon. She was still there when the present government of China took over control of the area. The hospital was taken over by the government but we understand Dr. Cheung was retained on the staff. For reasons of her personal safety, all contact with her was broken off at that time...[6]

The story in our bones

Others, men and women, have similar stories from Angola, Korea, Japan. Like us, they found themselves in foreign territory where they were sometimes shown little sympathy. They did not, however, yearn for the old ways. They just invented ways to survive and serve.

They could do this because they knew their story – the Jesus story – so well they were not threatened by the strangeness around them. They had no fears that their Christian identity would be somehow compromised.

They didn't need to declaim it to ears that didn't want to hear, because it was so in their bones that every action they undertook was an illumination of the Christ-spirit within. Hockin listening, interpreting, trying to yank the Western churches into understanding China's need for land reform, the vast shifts that led to revolution. Cheung, quietly, passionately healing, focused entirely on her vocation.

They did precisely the task that is ours today. Like Cheung and Hockin, we need to do three things:

• *Analyze and understand the context* in which we are living, congregation by congregation. While some issues are similar across the continent, others are very local.

• *Carry the Good News* (that all are loved by God, that grace abounds) in our blood and our bones. Offer it in a way that the people outside the church doors, as well as those within, can hear. Permit those who are just outside to eavesdrop on a fascinating conversation between a congregation and their God.

• *Bring healing.* And not just for ourselves. At the beginning of a new millennium, we are aware that the earth itself is as deeply in need of regeneration as a leper in Jesus' day. We need to heal the hurting body of Creation itself.

To do all this, we need to know who we are very well indeed. We cannot do evangelism if we do not feed ourselves with prayer and fellowship, with worship that leads us into mystery, and with ritual that sustains us at a very deep level. Our lives as communities of Christ have to be so filled with joy that anyone can see we have marvelous Good News.

What the Good News looks like today

Here's another letter. This one is from the Rev. Dawn Vaneyk, a minister in Sudbury, Ontario. She's the busy mother of a young child, Isaac; she is skilled in the art of meditation; and she serves a congregation that is having extraordinary fun teaching each other the Good News. She writes:

I haven't had a chance to see [the movie] "Prince of Egypt" yet, but by a lovely coincidence it came out just as I launched into my annual "Epic" sermon series, on Moses this year. (Did Joseph in six weeks last year.) I opt out of the lectionary between Epiphany and Lent to preach one of the great epics. The kids especially love it!

But several, including the Jr. Choir, have gone to see it. The director of the Jr. Choir has read the story to them as well, and they will be joined by some adults to put on the musical "Moses and the Freedom Fanatics" at the end of February.

It's been a challenge! There aren't a lot of sermon resources out there for preaching on Ten Plagues and a Passover. Last Sunday we had to cover nine chapters of Exodus in one blow! I brought in some of my son's toys — snakes, frogs, a magic wand (for Pharoah's sorcerers), plastic flies, and grasshoppers, etc. I have simply too much fun!

This week will be a little more merciful, with only a parting of seas, a drowning army, and a victory dance.

*The kids **love** the story. There's such wonderful stuff — water from the rock, Ten Commandments, a golden calf, and the daughters of Zelophehad. The story of a community learning to become a community again.*

The first story was one of the best: Isaac wore his Superman costume and we talked about superheroes, and were there any girl superheroes? We talked about the midwives, Miriam, Jochebed, and Pharoah's daughter as superheroes. I saw God at the burning bush as Mother/Grandmother — who else tells you to take off your shoes, you're standing on my shiny floor?[7]

Such joy! Such enthusiasm — a word which originally meant "filled with the spirit."

The people outside the church door — the uncommitted, the fabled "seekers" who have a hunger for the faith, but scarcely know what they are looking for — are finding their way to this delighted congregation. The doors are opening inwards — wide enough for people to come in. And at the same time they are opening outwards — for people to go out to meet the community around them, as Vaneyk describes in another letter:

Last weekend we staged "The Best Christmas Pageant Ever" to sellout crowds, with the last performance being on Sunday afternoon.

We're preparing now for our Hanukah observation. The Grade 2–3 class spent two Sundays learning about Hanukah and last Sunday made latkes! They'll recite the blessings (even trying a few Hebrew words) and will light the Hanukah candles.

Other cool Christmas plans that have come to fruition are the gifts that have made it to the Nursing Home, two families I know of finding people from the Nursing Home to be guests for Christmas Dinner, and the Sunday school having purchased the food for a Christmas feast to be held at a school in one of our lower income neighborhoods, where one of our women teaches Kindergarten. The kids went out and bought the provisions, volunteers cooked, and apparently the dinner was a great success. This was the kids' idea. It's fun to see them grow with a sense of compassion and mission.

Of course there's bad news with some deaths and serious illness threatening lives, and military strikes… But I look around me in this parish and I see starlight and holiness and I will not give in to "the boots of the tramping warriors."[8]

Make a joyful noise!

Look at all that's going on in that congregation:

- *Attention to the biblical story,* with all its color, including a Hanukah cele-bration. In the midst of Christmas, they both remind themselves of the long deep roots of their faith, and pay respect to the faith of others.
- *Drama,* lots of it, because the story comes alive if you are in the middle of it; not just sitting in a pew. And because today's people (the ones we are trying to reach, the ones seeking the Good News) aren't used to sitting still and being talked at.
- *Doors opening inward,* as people discuss and discover new insights into the biblical story that they share.
- *Doors opening outward,* with the congregation (the Sunday school stu-dents) going out to serve those in need.
- Above all, *a refusal* (similar to that of Hockin and Cheung) *to deny the pain of the world,* coupled with her assurance that "starlight and holiness" will always be stronger than the "boots of the tramping warriors."

All this, in many different forms, happens in congregations throughout this continent, fueled by imagination and love. It is the great strength of congregations that – supported by one other – they can sometimes look around bravely, sing the Good News, and bring healing. It is an evangelism we can undertake even after the residential schools, after ethnic cleansing, even after the Holocaust.

In this evangelism:

- We *know* the Jesus story (and the stories Jesus knew, like that of Moses and of Judah Macabee) in our bones.
- We *teach* these stories to each other with joy and excitement, knowing that they are the stories of our ancestors. They tell us who we are and keep us sane. They will help us, as Hockin was helped, to survive in tough times.
- We *go out* into a secular world serenely able to carry Jesus' spirit in such a way that people will say, "See, how they love one another," whenever they speak of our Christian communities.

- And (on our way out), we *fling those church doors wide open*, so that people can see inside and recognize the love and excitement and joy that is there. And can come closer.

What people don't want to hear

My friend, witnessing to Jehovah, went door to door saying things people didn't want to hear. Even if that's not our form of evangelism today, we still have to say the hard words – the words people don't always want to hear – and risk having doors shut in our faces, because of the gospel that commands us.

This does not mean giving up our own convictions. The problem with traditional evangelism is not that we have convictions, but that we have not allowed room for others to have convictions too.

Shortly before I started writing these chapters, my spouse had been hired as a denominational staff person here in the northern Ontario region where we live. One of his first tasks was to participate in an open forum about poverty in the area. He did so with considerable vigor, pointing out the specific nature of poverty in his small city, naming its causes in government cutbacks, and decrying in some detail the "politics of resentment" that had emerged in his province. He provided analysis and context.

And he deliberately chose theological language to name the rising homelessness, the increased attendance at food banks, the blatant punishment of the poor. When the local newspaper gave his remarks front-page coverage, he received a flurry of notes, phone calls, and visits – some approving, some sharply disapproving.

He then spent a large amount of time healing: talking at length to every person who approached him in anger, trying to "bring people together" in this situation. By the Cuban theologian Rene Castellanos' definition, he was doing evangelism.

Evangelism today still speaks the words of the gospel. Depending on where your congregation is located, those words sound something like this:

- *Blessed are you who are poor.* We know you need welfare at levels that will allow you to have enough to feed your children and take part in pizza days at school.
- *Blessed are you who are hungry now.* We know food banks are not enough, but we will offer them in a way that allows dignity, and we will try to elect people who want to offer a decent minimum wage to people too scared to agitate for better pay.
- *Blessed are you who weep.* We will not abandon you, and we will not blame you. We will sit with you, until you are capable of standing on your own again.
- *Blessed are you when people hate you, and when they exclude you, revile you, and defame you, on account of the Son of Man.*[9] Welcome to the club. If you're doing Jesus' work, under any label, we are with you.

Singing Jesus' song our way

We can respect others' convictions without yielding to them. Many people are unwilling to listen to other religions, fearing, perhaps, that listening automatically equates to agreement. But refusing to uphold and reach out with our own convictions is, in its own way, just as arrogant and unilateral a decision as imposing our beliefs and convictions on others.

We don't have to choose *either* theirs *or* ours. It can be *both* theirs *and* ours. We should *all* be free to express what we believe.

Singing the songs of Jesus as powerfully as our elders did, but in our own way, is a big order. We address it throughout this book, and of course, there are many more fine books about ways to do it. But in summary, here are some ways we tell the Good News, as congregations, in our local communities:

- *Understanding the temper of the times.* For instance, people today are distrustful of all large institutions. Shrinking attendance in churches is matched at Kiwanis, the Masonic Lodge, and symphony concerts. And because our institution – the church – is human, it will inevitably disappoint. While we might wish that we would have no clergy who embark on sexual harassment, for example, we will. We need to acknowledge sin and error when it happens and seek restoration.

That is evangelism, sharing the Good News.

- *Talking to each other.* People, both in and outside the church, who are uneasy with the nature of myth, history, scripture may confuse our reverence for our story with an inability to sort out fiction and science, truth and wisdom. But we all need small groups where we can offer our doubts and stories of faith to each other – where we learn to live gracefully with contradiction and ambiguity. These don't have to be Bible study groups, although that's one good approach. It happens in choir practice sometimes, at Church Council meetings, Sunday school teachers' meetings, pastoral care courses.

That is evangelism, sharing the Good News.

- *Hearing what's beneath an outsider's hesitation.* Many people, in and outside the church, are stressed, stretched by their jobs, exhausted. And some have reason to fear any church. For many years I watched a woman who wanted to come to a dream group offered by our congregation (but whose own experience in church as a child had been very hard) force herself to walk through the church door each meeting. She came because we had something she wanted so badly she would cross a threshold of painful memory to get there. We understood, and loved her for her courage.

That is evangelism, sharing the Good News.

- *Learning the language of the people.* That might mean a certain dying to self. Perhaps we will allow a new kind of music into church. A drum, a sax, instead of always an organ. In interfaith settings we will be equally attentive to the convictions of others as to our own. We will by turn speak, and – listening carefully to the words of others – be silent.

That is evangelism, sharing the Good News.

- *Offering respect.* The days of proselytizing are long past. We need to assume that the people hearing our words, or observing our deeds, are wise enough to understand what they mean. We will happily explain our motivations, if they ask. We are not ashamed of our beliefs. But we will not force our explanations down their throats, like stuffing a pill into a cat. We need to treat others with the same respect that we would treat ourselves.

That is evangelism, sharing the Good News.

- *Balancing hard words with soft ones.* Prophecy and pastoral care are both part of the Jesus story. Singing his song means we struggle for the same delicate balance he found, always trying to bring people closer together – the politicians and the impoverished, corporate bosses and unemployed, single moms and seniors. Whether it is the potluck supper or the symbolic feast of bread and wine, bringing people closer together is the strength of the congregation.

That is evangelism, sharing the Good News.

Harmony with God

CHRISTOPHER WHITE

*"I would have sent you away with mirth and songs,
with tambourine and lyre… Come now, let us make a
covenant, you and I; and let it be a witness
between you and me."*
Genesis 31:27b, 44

*[Jacob] bought for 100 pieces of money the plot
on which he had pitched his tent. There he raised an altar and
called it El-Elohe-Israel.*
Genesis 33:19–20

The church exists to worship God. Jacob's first act, on settling near Shechem, was to set up an altar for worshipping his God.

In our congregations today, the center of our being, the reason for our existence, is God, and Jesus Christ is our window into God.

During worship, we are God's people gathered together, praying, singing, hearing, and responding to the Word of God. Hopefully, we emerge

186 > JACOB'S BLESSING

refreshed and energized for the challenges that we face as we serve the mission of the church. Without our worship of God, we are simply a social service club – and not a very efficient one, at that.

Yet, if worshipping God is our defining characteristic, it is also the source of our greatest conflict. Worship wars have broken out across North America as the church responds to decline with an attempt to be relevant in its worship. The battle lines seem to be drawn between two opposing camps: those who wish to introduce contemporary worship, and those who want to maintain classical roots. The arguments are passionate, because in worship we reveal our concept of God, and God is something we feel very deeply.

Who do all these people say that I am?

The battle lines are not strictly over God. God is, by a kind of reverse definition, beyond our defining. So the battle lines usually form over Jesus, whom we believe to be the human revelation or incarnation of God. Who Jesus was, what he said or did not say, who he was or believed himself to be, has been the subject of intense debate and discussion during the past decade. The emergence of the Jesus Seminar and writers such as Dominic Crossan, Marcus Borg, and John Shelby Spong has set off a vigorous debate with other scholars such as John P. Meier, N.T. Wright, and Luke Timothy Johnston. The discussions have, until now, been quite polarized, their positions seemingly irreconcilable.

I think it's appropriate to look not where the scholarship has been, but rather where it is going. Because that may well tell us about how we will worship God in coming years.

In his book *Surpassing Wonder, The Invention of the Bible and the Talmuds,* historian Donald Harman Akenson uses A.A. Milne's *Winnie the Pooh* as a metaphor to describe what has happened to much biblical scholarship this decade. In one scene, Piglet and Pooh go around in circles following their own ever increasing number of footprints. (Cartoonist Walt Kelly borrowed the image for his comic strip *Pogo,* leading to the popular saying, "We have seen the enemy, and he is us!")

Scholars, Akenson suggests, may have fallen into the same trap:

The more one immerses oneself in the continually growing literature concerning the Historical Yeshua [Jesus], the more one realizes how dependent emotionally and cognitively the scholars are on each other, and how comforted they are by the ever growing band of footprints that fill their path. Certainly [they conclude] the quarry must be just ahead.[1]

He argues strongly that much of today's writing on the historical Jesus is open to question on the grounds of academic methodology:

With very few exceptions, the… practices of the historians of Yeshua, despite their best efforts, have not been those of sound historical practice… The vulnerability of the biblical historian under pressure leads to appeals to scholarly consensus as a mode of documenting propositions that ultimately should rest not on any secondary literature, or upon certain ideas commonly held, but upon primary sources and upon their rigorous interpretation.[2]

Old Testament scholar and pastoral minister Karen Hamilton echoes some of these concerns. As a theological centrist, Hamilton is concerned that some current scholarship, by prioritizing what Jesus may or may not have actually said, creates a canon within the canon of scripture and builds a hierarchy of texts.

"We need to be less arrogant when we engage the Bible," says Hamilton. "We assume a cultural superiority that is not warranted." As chair of the committee that produced the United Church of Canada's Interfaith document, *Bearing Faithful Witness* – which recognizes the traditional anti-Semitism of Christianity – Hamilton is very sensitive to how we treat scripture.

There is a belief that the liberal deconstructionist assumption is the last authority. It is one way of interpretation, not "the" way. We have been taught, for example, that when a line is repeated in the Bible, it's a scribal error, a mistake. It may not be a mistake; it may be deliberate. Why do we assume it's a mistake? Deliberate choices have been made by the writer. The question is, "What are they trying to tell us?"[3]

Her approach shifts the focus from accident – or worse, distortion – to intentionality. It may well lead us out of the current morass of contradictions in which we find ourselves. Currently, differences in the gospel accounts are used as "proof" that this or that, did or did not happen. By changing the question to "What are they trying to tell us?" we engage Jesus in a refreshing way. For instance, instead of dwelling on the differences between the gospel of John and the synoptic gospels, we might ask ourselves, "What is John trying to tell us about Jesus by having a very different chronology in his gospel from the synoptics'?"

When Europeans first reached North America, they treated the indigenous residents as a primitive people. They dismissed the richness of Native spirituality. Five hundred years later, we sometimes treat the writers of the Bible the same way, as simple people who understood neither the stars nor quantum physics. This attitude makes it too easy for us to dismiss the biblical witness.

For too long we have concentrated on the dissonance of scripture. It is time to listen for its harmonies.

Seeking harmony in different notes

Much of the current discussion seems to be framed around the question of who's right and who's wrong. Fortunately, there are signs that we are moving in a very different direction. Marcus Borg and N. T. Wright are scholars who, on the surface, appear to take totally opposite sides when it comes to Jesus. But while they differ significantly, they have together produced a thoughtful dialogue between their positions. In *The Meaning of Jesus: Two Visions,* Borg and Wright attempt to reframe the debate. While acknowledging their differences, they say:

Where we do agree, however, is on the following point. Debate about Jesus has recently been acrimonious, with a good deal of name calling and angry polemic in both public and private discourse.[4]

There may never be agreement. But the book demonstrates that we can live and worship as one, even when we embrace a different paradigm of the biblical reality. Respect amidst diversity gives us a model for how we can worship together.

And there is probably no area of church life where people cling more tightly to their personal preferences than worship, and no area where we need respect more.

Confirmation Sunday

The electric guitar and the drums vibrated the walls of the sanctuary. The sounds flooded out the windows, into the parking lot, and through the whole surrounding neighborhood.

Showing my advanced age, I charged to the front and told the band, "Turn that down! The people will be blasted out of their pews and into outer space at that volume!"

With a tad of reluctance, the band turned down the amplifiers.

It was Confirmation Sunday. We had, for the first time, an electrified band and our organist playing together. We sang biblically based choruses along with "Amazing Grace," "I, the Lord of Sea and Sky," and "Joyful, Joyful." The 11 young people being confirmed had developed the service, and were leading it. They read the prayers and the scripture; they acted out liturgical drama. It was a long, somewhat chaotic, and gloriously imperfect service – but the youth left feeling ten feet tall and truly included.

They were there that Sunday because they wanted to be. They were involved. They were not just spectators.

Drop-out day

I don't know what you remember about your confirmation, but I remember one primary emotion – an incredible feeling of freedom. Now that I was confirmed, I wouldn't have to go to church anymore!

In many of our churches, Confirmation Sunday is Graduation Day. That's the day when – if they haven't left us already – the youth of the church begin emotionally and physically to move out of congregational life. In the mainline church we passively accept this departure. We comfort ourselves: "Well, what can you expect at that age?" We reassure ourselves: "When they get older, when they start a family, they'll be back."

Wait! Think about that assumption for minute. Assume those young folks are confirmed at 14 or 15. They get married in their late 20s. They start a family in their early 30s. Simple arithmetic tells us that by that time, they will have been absent from our congregations for more than half their lives! And then we expect them to return?

Let's be blunt. We failed them, and we failed ourselves. We expected them to constantly adjust to our culture, without ever attempting to adjust to theirs. No wonder they left.

We have been fortunate over the past decade. A small portion of those former youth did come back to church. A very small portion of the biggest population surge of this century. If we could really depend on our adult children coming back to church, we should have been swamped. We weren't.

But the boomer generation is entering the end of its child-bearing cycle. Sheer demographics will mean fewer baptisms, fewer children in Sunday school, and larger numbers moving through youth groups and out. We are likely to have a replay of the 1970s. Formerly thriving congregations will once again be empty of children and youth, and will wonder once again if they have a future.

In the chapter on Sunday schools, I wrote about the dearth of boys in our classes. The weakness of our current system of Christian education was all too evident in our latest confirmation class. Of the 11 young people confirmed, only one was male.

Interestingly enough, at the youth drop-in center we help to run, we have the opposite problem. There are more boys than girls. What can we do to deal with this imbalance? How can we keep our youth active and involved?

The clash of cultures

Once again, the current ranges of answers tends towards polarities, towards mutually contradictory extremes.

For some the answer is clear: we must change our whole worship service to retain our youth. The needs and interests of one age group must take priority over all other groups. For the proponents of this view, worship needs to become "culturally relevant." It is an attractive argument – but we need to ask, "Whose culture?" And who is defining it for us?

In fact, every congregation is multicultural. Merely having different generations worshipping together guarantees that. The culture of our elders was the postwar world. It's very different from the culture of my generation. And the culture of my children is as radically different from mine, as mine is from my parents. Yet we all worship together. So how, then, do we meet the differing worship needs of each generation? Do we sacrifice all the other cultures in favor of one target audience? Do we attempt to blend cultures?

Some, at the other extreme, suggest we shouldn't even try. Bill Easum, in his seminal book *Dancing with Dinosaurs,* argues in favor of what I think of as "liturgical ghettoes."

Aging congregations cannot be expected to give up a style of worship that fits their culture in order to reach the younger generations. Neither is it fair to ask younger generations to worship in the culture of the older generation. It is much easier to start a separate and distinct worship service.[5]

He's correct – it would be easier. But I don't think it's right.

Last weekend we had a family barbecue. Three generations of my family gathered together at our house. Our home buzzed with activity. Teens, preteens, toddlers, babies, parents, and grandparents were all eating, talking, arguing, and playing together. We didn't segregate ourselves, generation by generation. We were a family, and there was rich interplay among all ages and stages.

Nor did we set separate tables for every generation: children and youth outside, grandparents in the basement, boomers at the dining table, Generation-Xers in the kitchen. I would find that an appalling image. Yet that's what we seem quite content to do when we create separate "alternative worship" environments for each of our generations.

A church dominated by the demographic needs of one generation is not a church, it's a marketing exercise. A colleague from the Christian Reform tradition told me this story:

A congregation in my denomination went enthusiastically into alternative worship. It appeared the ideal solution. The older folks didn't want modern music and the younger ones were tired of the old hymns. So the early service became the worship for young families and the 11:00 a.m. worship was populated by more senior people.

As the attendance patterns became more entrenched, identity was formed, not on the basis of belonging to the church, but on the service in which people participated. What evolved was essentially two different churches, sharing the same building.

When a congregational meeting was held on a property matter, the church was split down the middle according to which worship was attended. There was no agreement and no common ground. They didn't even speak the same language.

The only way found to break the impasse was to reformulate worship. The services were blended; everyone was able to experience each other, and a sense of full community was restored. By being willing to give something up, and by listening to the others, much more was gained. The church was restored.

It's not only about the sermon!

I could devote most of this chapter to the role and nature of sermons, because I love and believe in preaching. Sermons can be a point of division between the cultures and the generations. For some – particularly if they come from a tradition that puts high emphasis on preaching – the sermon is their primary reason for coming to church. For others, especially the younger members, it can be the part of the service they like least, an unpleasant interlude they have to force themselves to sit through. For a generation accustomed to interactive computer programs, fast paced videos, and multimedia presentations, a sermon can appear to be an anachronism, a throwback to the communication styles of several centuries ago.

But it doesn't need to be that way.

A number of years ago I was standing up in the pulpit preaching on a Sunday morning. I was at the halfway mark when I realized that the rest of my sermon notes were back in the office. I had a number of choices before me. I could say "Amen" and announce another hymn. I could flee the pulpit, rummage through my office, and hope that no one noticed my absence. Instead, I chose to continue, reconstructing the sermon as best I could.

As I spoke without notes, a number of things happened. First, I had real eye contact with the people in the pews. I knew right away what was working and what was losing their interest. Second, I remembered the rest of the sermon; it was sitting right there in my mind waiting to be preached. I didn't need my notes as much as I thought I did. The door response was instructive as well. People loved the immediacy of the experience, and the fact that I was looking right at them.

Over the years my preaching has evolved from that Sunday.

I now rarely use notes. This puts a lot of emphasis on preparation and rehearsal. If I don't start at the first of the week, the results will not be the quality I want to share with my congregation.

I also preach from a small platform at the front of the sanctuary. I come down to the people, rather then have the people look up at me. That in itself sends a significant message.

My preaching is by no means perfect – nobody bats .1000! There are times when I finish the sermon and suddenly realize that I have left out an important point – which I then slip into the pastoral prayer! But aside from those times when absolute precision is required, I never go back to the pulpit or to notes.

Preaching has gone in and out of fashion like the width of neckties, but it will always have an important place in the life of the church. If done properly, with humility and hard work, it can touch people's lives in a unique way. When the young man in **Blessing 8,** on ministry, came to see me, his visit was triggered by a sermon. Regularly, people come to me for help or pastoral counseling as a result of a sermon.

Preaching will continue to be important, as a place to tell the biblical story, to tell stories of faith, and as a place to teach theology, both classic and contemporary, and to share the broad spectrum of biblical scholarship.

We may see the re-emergence of series preaching as a way to work through themes and continuous stories outside of the lectionary. What I wrote in **Blessing 6,** on Sunday schools, also applies to preaching. The lectionary will continue to be the main format used by the church. There are so many wonderful resources that are available, including Internet sites such as Richard Fairchild's "Preaching and Lectionary Resources" site, that it would be foolish to abandon it completely. However, we should not always feel bound by its constructs, and there will be times when we move away from it to enhance the richness of the biblical story.

I also believe in the appropriate use of humor in sermons. Conrad Hyers, in *The Comic Vision and the Christian Faith,* wrote that "humor is not the opposite of seriousness; humor is the opposite of despair." North American culture tends to use humor as a crude weapon, to denigrate and attack others. But Jesus was joyful; he loved being with people, sharing food and community. My favorite picture of him is the drawing by the late Willis Wheately that shows Jesus with his head thrown back and laughter on his face. Laughter can be healing, and humor, used judiciously, makes a point in a way that nothing else can.

Good preaching also needs to come from the bottom up, rather than the top down. By that I mean the preacher needs to do a lot of listening during the week. Listening to the concerns of the people, what is touching their lives, where they hurt. We need to remember that anyone can preach, but it is a privilege to earn the right to be heard. When the spoken word integrates scripture with the real world of people's lives, then both the preacher and the people can be transformed.

For the future of preaching I strongly recommend the books by Paul Wilson, professor of preaching at Emmanuel College in Toronto and the editor of the preaching journal *Word and Witness*. Wilson is a leading scholar and proponent of preaching, and his books are in use across North America.

Much as I enjoy preaching, we preachers need to realize that the sermon is only part of the worship experience. In biblical times, the Jewish people had three forms of worship. There were the family liturgies, such as the Passover Seder. There were the grand rituals at the Temple in Jerusalem, performed on behalf of the people by the high priests. And there were the synagogues, where the scrolls of the scriptures were read and interpreted. Our Sunday worship services attempt to combine all three in one event. Some Temple rituals are done by the priest or ordained minister on behalf of the people, such as baptism. The family rituals become Communion, the sharing of bread and wine, for example, or responsive litanies including hymns and songs. And the sermon takes the place of teaching in the synagogues.

The shape and style of the sermon depends on the rest of the worship experience. What we preach, and how we preach it, will be influenced by our understanding of God, of Jesus, and of the community we belong to.

A good sermon will never be enough to salvage poor worship; conversely, a weak sermon will not destroy good worship. The *worship* is paramount.

Taking music as the model

Another way to explore our understanding of worship is through the music we choose to play and sing.

Once again, there are two major competing visions about music polarizing our worship life. Tragically, music is one of the greatest sources of division we face in congregations. My editor for this book, Jim Taylor, was for 15 years editor of the clergy journal *pmc: the Practice of Ministry in Canada.* He told me that one subject sure to provoke spirited discussion in the journal's editorial board was conflict over music policy. But in those 15 years, the journal never published an issue on relationships of clergy with organists or choir directors – the subject was just too hot to handle!

The reasons for conflict seem clear: a combination of panic, entrenched opinions, changing musical tastes, lack of collegiality, and a lack of appreciation of all sides.

Church consultant Bill Easum takes the clergy's side:

The source of the conflict comes primarily from trained musicians who…resist any change in the style of music. Church musicians do more to hinder congregations from sharing new life than any other staff members. Many are more interested in music appreciation then in helping people find new life. They are musicians first and worship leaders second. Their love for music rivals their love for Christ. Making disciples is not as important as making good music.[6]

Those are strong words.

In the beautiful old sanctuary of Metropolitan United Church in Toronto, a glorious organ fills the chancel with the opening chords to *Phantom of the Opera.* The visiting high school sits entranced at the power of the instrument. The organist, Patricia Wright, speaks with passion to the gathered teenagers. A whole new world is opening up for them.

Later, I meet with her and her colleague, the Rev. Malcolm Sinclair. They are a remarkable team, a model of collegiality and mutual respect.

I asked Wright for her reaction to Easum's words. "Hurtful," she replied succinctly. "It's hurtful to read that. It's also a sweeping generalization and a stereotype. Most organists are not like that."

Patricia Wright thinks music has become the scapegoat for anything that's not working well in the church: "Many in the church want instant change and believe that music as entertainment will fill the pews. It's just not that simple."

She also is concerned by the lack of collegiality she sees in many ministerial teams. "Organists feel unappreciated and isolated," she told me.

Malcolm Sinclair agrees with her assessment. "It's important that we, as colleagues, support one another publicly," he says. Sinclair also feels that much contemporary music in worship has missed a central point: "The music serves the biblical text. Great music adds mystery to our worship; it links us to the church's tradition and history. The first 20 bars of the St. Anne Fugue in E# is a message from their world to our world."

Poor music means poor worship

Both Sinclair and Wright believe that poor music means poor worship, something the church can ill afford.

For both of them, social action comes out of worship. Worship empowers people to go into the world. As an inner city downtown church that has both a thriving worshipping congregation, combined with a phenomenal outreach program, Metropolitan stands as a living contradiction to those who believe that without "praise music" congregations will inevitably decline.

Sinclair and Wright are not content to sit idly by and witness the conflict they see around them. Instead, they lead workshops on how clergy and musicians can work together in harmony. Using the metaphor of wearing each other's hats, they show how to build a relationship based upon mutual respect and understanding.

When Neil MacQueen went to Barrington, Illinois, his Presbyterian church was struggling in the shadow of Willow Creek, the ultimate megachurch. MacQueen and Barrington made a conscious decision to create a strong traditional church. Traditional music and preaching worked together, reinforcing each other. The church grew with each passing year and was transformed into a thriving congregation.

There is no single way to worship and thrive. The music, the preaching, the liturgy, all must work together in harmony to have effective and inspiring worship.

Two way street

My spouse is a trained classical singer who has sung in church choirs since she was 13. When I announced to her, in the early 1980s, that I wanted to enter the ordained ministry, I was taken aback at her very negative reaction. I had unwittingly chosen the one line of work that ranked absolutely lowest on her list of potential spousal occupations.

As we worked through this together, it became apparent why she felt this way. From the moment she joined the church choir as a young teenager, she saw how ministers were ridiculed and joked about by choir members and music directors alike. The clergy were given little respect; some choir members even read books during the sermons! She saw me entering a life where, in her eyes, I would be constantly ridiculed by the people I had to work most closely with.

One of my responses to this has been to always sing in the choir. I find that participation helps both parties understand much more clearly each other's issues and concerns. Singing in the choir ensures that I am not just a faceless backview to the choir, and they are not just noises behind my back to me. And I must say that in my ministry I have been shown only respect and courtesy by the organists with whom I have ministered.

The right emphasis

Marva Dawn, a Lutheran lay person, church musician, and theologian has waded into the worship wars with her own book, *Reaching Out Without Dumbing Down.*[7] Dawn believes that much of contemporary worship misses the key point – that God is the center of our worship. (That's why our understanding of Jesus, which I referred to earlier, is crucial.) Much of contemporary worship, she believes, moves God to the sidelines. It focuses solely on the experience of the worshipper.

"Praise worship," she asserts, let's us see only one side of our relationship with God:

"Praise" that uses only upbeat songs can be extremely destructive to worshippers because it denies the reality of doubts concerning God, the hiddenness of God, and the feelings of abandonment by God that cloud believers going through difficult times... Many question their faith because they are not able to be as happy as their fellow believers. They can't enter into upbeat worship if their lives are in shambles... To be only upbeat is to be unbiblical. In post-modern escapism, it also ignores the immense suffering of the world.[8]

Worship of the "don't worry, be happy" mindset is a sugar-coated placebo meant to make us feel better without coming close to addressing the complexity of our relationship to God and the real daily struggles of human life.

No technological solutions

Wherever I go, I hear enthusiasts arguing that we need to embrace the new technologies available to us, to modernize our worship. Consider the implications of this excerpt from William Easum and Tom Bandy in *Growing Spiritual Redwoods.* Worship, they say, will be

- Visual! Printed reading material will be cut back or entirely eliminated. Words, songs, pictures, images, and symbols will be projected in color throughout the service. Television monitors, LCD projectors, holographic replicators, and other odd equipment will regularly insert moving pictures into worship.
- Surround Sound! Sound systems will be state of the art, amplified and surround worship participants. Music and sound effects will form a continuous background to worship.
- Technology supported! Computers, video cameras and monitors, sound mixers, electronic keyboards and synthesizers will be used by trained volunteer technological support teams. Computer stations at tables or seats in the congregation will directly link participants with worship leaders...[9]

If World Vision's survey of Canadian congregations is correct, two-thirds of Canadian churches have 125 or fewer worshippers in them on Sunday mornings.[10] How are congregations of that size going to have the people or financial resources to provide the Easum/Bandy vision, even assuming that they wanted to?

And probably they shouldn't. Marva Dawn believes that the destructive power of television has addicted us to entertainment:

Technicization destroys human skills for intimacy…the speed, mobility, and fragmentation of modern life leave most persons desperately hungry for the very intimacy they do not know how to create. Even more deadly is the sense that we can solve all our problems with technological advances, that we are masters of our destiny. This aggravates the already prevailing rejection of God, institutions, and authority that characterizes the modern cosmology.[11]

Jim Taylor, in his Internet column *Edges*[12], made an even more disturbing point. He noted a parallel between the technology of weapons and the technology of words. Just as weapons have evolved from hand-to-hand combat to guided missiles that can be fired at unknown and invisible targets from 30,000 feet, so have words gone from face-to-face communication to prerecorded statements delivered through a camera, a computer, or a printing press to an unknown and invisible audience. The increasing use of technology in worship, he suggests, makes the people in the pews into audience – or worse, into targets – rather than worshippers.

Is our worship to be completely contextual, arising only out of the perceived needs of the dominant demographic group? Or are we to create a haven from technology, contemporary music, and "feel good" emotions?

I find neither option palatable.

God loves diversity

The solution, I believe, lies in an openness to diversity in our worship. Diversity does not mean division. You do not achieve compromise by moving to multi-services. Rather, diversity means acknowledging that no one style, neither contemporary nor classical, holds the absolute "truth," but that there are many ways to worship and celebrate our living God.

For worship to be authentic, in my view, it must first be multigenerational. The whole family should be around the table.

There also needs to be a willingness on the part of each member of the body of Christ to give up something for the sake of the whole. Sacrifice is not a popular word or concept in this new century; it does not go well with the immediate self-gratification that seems to be our current hallmark. But I suspect it's an idea whose time has come again. The future, I firmly believe, lies in blended worship, an exciting fusion of past, present, and future musical styles.

All congregations say that they want to attract new people and keep the young. But they fall, in my experience, into two main types. The difference between the two has nothing to do with their style of worship, and everything to do with their attitude and focus.

One type says all the right things, but has an underlying message that overpowers that sentiment: "We want to grow, as long as the new people are just like us and will fit into our way of doing things."

These churches have never left the green oasis of Elim. Their attitude is clear – they would rather die than change. They block any innovation or new life with either active or passive resistance. Although they do attract new members, after a few months, people with energy and vision give up and leave. This secretly delights the church, which can then return to their comfortable lament about this new faithless generation.

The second type of church deals with the struggle of balancing the old and the new. They are genuinely concerned with the needs of all in their community. They live with the creative tension and uncertainty. They recognize that there is no one answer to all the challenges, there is simply the journey of faith. They honor the past, while moving into the future. They are able to discern the difference between innovation and change for the sake of change; they do not panic; they are willing to risk and to fail. The individual members are willing to sacrifice their personal preferences for the health of the whole. They are willing to advance into the desert, in search of the promised land.

The second type of church will be with us for many years. I'd guess that the first has only five to eight years left.

More than musicians, ministers of music

The same distinction applies to worship leaders. When both clergy and musicians are willing to sacrifice for the health of the whole, something wonderful can happen.

In my ministry, I have been blessed with musicians who definitely fit into that group.

In Springbank, Alberta, when we hired our first paid music director, we were fortunate to have Dr. Jamie Syer living in our community. Jamie had a doctorate in piano performance from Yale University and modeled diversity. He had us singing Baroque cantatas written by Buxtehude as well as contemporary anthems and cantatas. He valued both equally and the music program grew rapidly, deepening our worship experience.

Ron Kellington at Westminster, was a church organist and choir director for over 50 years, before he retired in 1998. Raised in the classical tradition and with a deep love for that music, Ron was always collegial and willing to work with me on different musical ideas, whether it was helping out in the creation of a lay-led men's and women's chorus, our short-lived alternative service, or our multigenerational orchestra. Ron's concern was always the health of the church. He was always willing to try new innovations. And when we did not agree, we always worked out our differences with collegiality and mutual respect. He was a gift to the church.

Margaret Motum followed him last year. Margaret suggests that there are two types of music directors. Some are, she says,

always looking for that ideal choir, ideal organ, and ideal church. They will happily take a job anywhere, and the church doesn't affect them emotionally as it is just a job. The other wants to be a full member of the whole church. They are interested and committed to the congregation's whole ministry.

Margaret Motum believes passionately in musical diversity; she embraces the full spectrum of classical and contemporary church music. With Margaret we have sung all styles. And like her predecessor, she is involved in the full congregational life at Westminster.

This past Lent was an excellent example of what can be done. On Palm Sunday we had an intergenerational celebration service with music from our Senior Choir, our youth (singing an appropriate excerpt from their musical), and our children, backed up by the Westminster orchestra. For the first time, we added liturgical dance – it was both appropriate and moving. Using drama and preaching, the transitions from the joy of parade to the grief of betrayal were handled sensitively. It was a rich experience for all involved. We moved on to a very traditional Good Friday Cantata that deeply touched our hearts and illuminated the Passion narrative. Then we completed the cycle with the celebratory trumpet music of Easter. Attendance was the best we had ever experienced for Lent. In all these services, we were respecting and maintaining our tradition, while exploring new musical forms from around the globe.

We are not a huge richly endowed church. We are a mid-sized, "program size" church. Although some experts predict the imminent demise of congregations our size, here we stand.

You can too. It does not matter the size of your congregation or your community – there are talented people everywhere. Search the schools and the wider community for vocal groups, bands and other musicians. Look for actors and dramatists, for dancers and visual artists, especially in the fabric arts. They will come to worship with you and happily share their talents.

As I write this, we have a community girls' choir coming this Sunday. A few weeks from now a local Swing Band is joining us. In Vancouver, BC, St. Andrew's Wesley United Church has been holding jazz liturgies, and what began as an experiment is now drawing worshippers from all over the region. Hiding in many churches are talented musicians and performers who never thought that their talents were appropriate for church. Find them! They are a great resource.

Our worship is more complete when we understand that not only are the clergy and the musicians teammates, but that both work in concert with the congregation. Worship is the collective expression of the people's faith in God. Being open to, and using, their ideas in a collaborative relationship allows our expression of faith to reach its greatest potential.

Never make believe

The key to worship for me is integrity. The integrity of the music, the preaching, the drama. Whatever form it takes, we are there not to worship ourselves, but God. There is theatre in worship, but worship is not theatre.

If we are open to the Spirit, if we understand that God is constantly engaging us on different levels, then we can free ourselves from the artificial boundaries that have historically bound us. Our worship at its best connects us to God and takes us beyond human experience and into the Divine.

The church exists to worship God. For God's sake, let our worship truly reflect the God we know.

Closing Thoughts

Jacob was left alone;
and a man wrestled with him until daybreak.
(Genesis 32:24)

Now the boy Samuel was ministering to the LORD under
Eli. The word of the LORD was rare in those days;
visions were not widespread.
At that time Eli, whose eyesight had begun to grow
dim so that he could not see, was lying down in his room; the
lamp of the LORD had not yet gone out; and Samuel was
lying down in the temple of the LORD, where the ark of God
was. Then the LORD called, "Samuel! Samuel!" and he said,
"Here I am!" and ran to Eli.
1 Samuel 3:1–5a

God often comes to us in the dark, alone. Jacob dreams a great dream with his head on a strong stone; and later, by the edge of river, he wrestles with God. God's voice wakes Samuel from sleep.

These stories overflow with meaning. When we (in denominations that once could proudly talk to governments) feel that the dark surrounds us, we need to remember that is precisely when God comes to change the shape of history. The shepherds saw angels announcing Jesus' birth in the worst kind of dark, when Roman legions occupied the land. And Jacob wrestles with God, in the night, at a place where land and water meet – a threshold place. Things happen at such places, as they do where the mountain meets the sky.

And Samuel, late at night, alone in the temple with the ark. There should be a thousand exclamation points here. A child, unknowing, alone with the ark of God. Only two chapters later in the First Book of Samuel, the mere presence of the ark of God terrorized the people of Ashod and Ekron. Any who come near it were stricken. "Those who did not die were stricken with tumors, and the cry of the city went up to heaven," says the biblical account.[1]

We should not feel, then, that we are dealing a God who has no power. If God could come to a man of greed and cunning; if God could come to a young child, Samuel; and later, if God could come as the child Jesus to all the people of earth; then surely God will come to God's church.

In any case, the worst thing that could happen to us is not that the church will die. It is – as in Samuel's day – that we will lose the ability to dream. "The word of the LORD was rare in those days," the writer of the passage says bleakly. "Visions were not widespread."

So our task now is like that of Jacob, or even Samuel. We are on a vision quest in a time of few visions. We wait. And while we wait, we hone our faithfulness:

We try to teach the children the best way possible, testing and breaking apart our models of Sunday school, doing the finest job we can.

We revive the old ways of healing in our congregations, with a resident healer (the parish nurse) and prayer, and oil for anointing, and healing touch.

We sing lovingly, in whatever way we can. If the young make music one way and the old another, we learn to listen gently to each other. Our buildings will be full of many instruments, and joy.

We do not lose hope. As Sam Kobia of the National Council of Churches of Kenya says, speaking of his troubled, debt-ridden country "We are Christians. We are called to have hope rather than despair."

We pray.

We learn the stories of the faith, because they will always give us hope. They help us know as Eli knew (and shepherds near Bethlehem knew) when it is God's voice (or possibly God's angels) speaking in the dark.

We listen to the elders and without demanding they be saints. We have learned from Jacob and, later, from Matthew the tax collector, that God does not reserve God's presence only for the good.

Like Samuel, when we cannot recognize God's voice we go to the old ones. Like Jacob, we seek to be reconciled with those we have hurt.

Above all, we should consider the possibility that God is already reviving the church – we just can't see how God is doing it.

But if we pray and wait and listen, perhaps we will be like Samuel. When the Lord's voice is heard, we will at last recognize it. And we will say, "Speak, for your servant is listening."

If we pray and wait and listen, perhaps we will hear the voice of God. And then – if we are ready – we will cling to God with all our might. Like Jacob, we will say: "I will not let you go, unless you bless me."

And we will be blessed.

– **Donna Sinclair**

A few weeks ago, as I write these concluding thoughts, I was sitting in a worship service in St. Paul's Cathedral in London, England. It was the annual service for the Lord Mayor of London. The mayors of the surrounding boroughs and towns were gathered together under that famous dome. The music was glorious, the organ thundered, and as I looked around in that great cathedral that has seen so much history, I realized how important it was to the people of that teeming city.

Today, I attended worship at a little rural church near our family cottage. The church itself is located at the top of a ridge and is surrounded by fields and forests. The congregation is small. About a dozen of us, including two children and a baby, sit together in the lovely little sanctuary. But that little country church is also important to that rural community. I knew how hard they had struggled to keep it open.

The church – wherever it may be – is still important, not only for its ministry, but for what it symbolizes: a living God, and a way of being that challenges the principalities and powers of our time, and of every time.

But in this new century, what continues to draw people to worship? It's certainly not a societal expectation. Quite the opposite now. So I picked up the phone and called some of my congregation back home. I asked them: "Why do you go to church?" It wasn't a scientific poll, just a question to some people who attended most Sundays and represented all ages and stages on the journey of faith:

- "The church helps me to become the kind of person I want to be. The week just doesn't seem right unless I've been in church."
- "It's my way of life. Without God, I don't know what I'd do"
- "It helps me in my work in the criminal justice system; it allows me to understand the world better. It supports my values and helps how I feel I should be."
- "I love talking to other adults about ideas, about the sermon, and I love singing the music. It's something I look forward to."
- "Community spirit – I find religion in belonging to a faith community, in worshipping with my neighbor, in working together."
- "I want to pass the faith on to my children. The sense of community is very important to me. In church we're all together as a family. We have a lot of nice things in our life, and I don't think that God should be last on the list of activities."
- "It forces you to pay attention, and to ask questions: 'Why am I here?' 'Who is my God?' 'What am I to do?'"
- "The church is a window. In it, you first see a reflection of yourself, then it leads you to look outside, and finally, to move out into the world."
- "The church is the only place in our society where all ages and economic levels can mix together. It's the wellspring of moral

responsibility. If it disappeared, we would hardly recognize the society that would be left."

For myself, I go to church because without God I'm not a whole person. Part of me is missing. The way to find that God and become whole, for me, is in that worshipping community, the church. God is revealed in our worship, our outreach, our Sunday school, even our Board meetings. In that glorious and at times cantankerous church, God is revealed for me and to the world.

Bruce McLeod, a former Moderator of my denomination, asks a question: "If your church were to close, would the sidewalks in your community sag from lack of love?" I hope the answer is "yes" in all our communities, because our world needs the love of God urgently. God needs the church urgently to share that love.

There is much work for us to do, and we no longer have the luxury of pining for Elim, of dreaming of the past. We are called by God, as revealed in Jesus Christ, to serve others, to put aside our own concerns, and to look beyond our own walls. If we understand ourselves as a servant people, then I truly believe that we shall, like Jacob, prevail.

May it be so for our churches and congregations. May we all go forth, as God's people, to love and serve the world and discover the unique gifts and ministry that our churches have to offer. Thanks be to God for all that we shall become, and Amen.

– CHRISTOPHER WHITE

Footnotes

Introduction

[1] Reginald W. Bibby, *There's Got to be More! Connecting Churches & Canadians,* Winfield, BC: Wood Lake Books, 1995, p. 110.

[2] From Janet Weiblen, United Church of Christ, Wahpeton, ND, on <u>midrash@joinhands.com.</u>

Chapter 1

[1] Marcus J. Borg, *Meeting Jesus Again for the First Time: The Historical Jesus & the Heart of Contemporary Faith,* San Francisco: HarperSanFrancisco, 1994, p. 32 ff.

[2] Borg, p. 34.

[3] Loren B. Mead, *Transforming Congregations for the Future,* Bethesda, MD: Alban Institute, 1994, p. 1 ff. has an excellent discussion and statistical analysis of the decline of the mainline church.

[4] Bruce McLeod, *City Sermons: Preaching from a Downtown Church,* Burlington, ON: Welch Publishing, 1986, pp. 88–89.

[5] "Bearing Faithful Witness: United Church-Jewish Relations Today," *Record of Proceedings,* Toronto: The United Church of Canada, 1997, p. 45.

[6] Francis Fukuyama, "The Great Disruption: Human Nature and the Reconstitution of Social Order," *The Atlantic Monthly,* May 1999, p. 80.

Chapter 2

[1] George Soros, *The Crisis of Global Capitalism: Open Society Endangered,* New York: Public Affairs, Perseus Books Group, 1998, p. xx.

[2] William Wolman & Anne Colamosca, *The Judas Economy: The Triumph of Capital and the Betrayal of Work*, New York: Addison-Wesley, 1997, p. 1.

[3] Wolman & Colamosca. p. 5.

[4] Angus Reid, *Shakedown: How the New Economy is Shaping our Lives*, Toronto: Doubleday Canada, 1996, p. 191.

Chapter 3

[1] Reginald Bibby, *Unknown Gods: The Ongoing Story of Religion in Canada,* Toronto: Stoddart, 1993, p. 17.

[2] Rosemary Radford Ruether, *Gaia and God: An Ecofeminist Theology of Earth Healing*, New York: HarperCollins, 1992, p. 227.

[3] Ruether, p. 207.

[4] Esther de Waal, *Every Earthly Blessing: Celebrating a Spirituality of Creation,* Ann Arbor, MI: Charis, 1992, p. 13.

[5] de Waal, p. 22.

[6] de Waal, p. 74.

[7] "Towards a Thinking Faith," *The United Church Observer,* January 1995, p. 32.

[8] Bibby, *Unknown Gods,* p. 225.

[9] "Mending the World: An Ecumenical Vision for Healing and Reconciliation," *Record of Proceedings,* 36th General Council, Toronto: The United Church of Canada, 1997, p. 198.

[10] "Mending the World," p. 217.

[11] Sallie McFague, "New Ways to Describe God," in *pmc: The Practice of Ministry in Canada,* May 1996, p. 5.

Chapter 4

[1] Rochelle Graham, Wayne Irwin, and Flora Litt, *Healing from the Heart: A Guide to Christian Healing for Individuals and Groups,* Kelowna, BC: Wood Lake Books, 1998, p. 15.

[2] Graham, Irwin, and Litt, pp. 18–19.

[3] Jo Revill, "Widow's Anguish at 'fatal' 4-month wait for surgery," London: *The Evening Standard,* June 23, 1999, p. 5.

Chapter 5

[1] Reginald Bibby, *Unknown Gods:The Ongoing Story of Religion in Canada,* Toronto: Stoddart, 1993, p. 137.

[2] John W. Friesen, *You Can't Get There From Here:The Mystique of North American Plains Indians' Culture and Philosophy*, Dubuque, IO: Kendall/Hunt, 1995, p. 82.

[3] Friesen, p. 82.

[4] *Record of Proceedings,* 31st General Council, Toronto: The United Church of Canada, August, 1986, www.uccan.org/Healing.htm.

[5] *For Seven Generations: An Information Legacy of the Royal Commission on Aboriginal Peoples,* Ottawa: CD-Rom, Libraxus Inc., 1997 (Public Hearings, Ottawa, 93-11-08).

[6] *The United Church Observer,* October, 1986, p. 11.

[7] Nicholas Flood Davin, "Report on Industrial Schools," as quoted in *Shingwauk's Vision* by J.R. Miller, Toronto: University of Toronto Press, 1996, p. 102.

[8] Moderator's statement, Tuesday, October 27, 1998.

[9] Moderator's statement.

[10] Reginald Bibby, *Mosaic Madness:The Poverty and Potential of Life in Canada,* Toronto: Stoddart, 1990, p. 160.

[11] Bibby, *Mosaic Madness,* p. 161.

[12] Richard Wagamese, *A Quality of Light,* Toronto: Doubleday Canada, 1997, pp. 319 – 320.

[13] Bibby, *Unknown Gods,* p. 119.

[14] Bibby, *Unknown Gods,* p. 119.

[15] Friesen, p. 67.

[16] Friesen, p. 67.

Chapter 6

[1] Marva Dawn, *Reaching Out Without Dumbing Down: A Theology of Worship for the Turn of the Century Culture,* Grand Rapids: Eerdmans, 1995, p. 76.

[2] Anne Lamott, *Traveling Mercies: Some Thoughts on Faith,* New York: Pantheon Books, division of Random House, 1999, p. 99-100.

[3] Howard Gardner, "The Theory of Multiple Intelligences," from Robin Fogarty and James Bellanca, *Multiple Intelligences: A Collection,* Palatine, IL: IRI/Skylight, 1995, p. 80.

[4] Gardner, p. 82.

[5] Howard Gardner and Tomas Hatch, "Multiple Intelligences Go to School," from Robin Fogarty and James Bellanca, *Multiple Intelligences: a Collection,* Palatine, IL: IRI/Skylight, p. 152. Also see www.ed.uri.edu/homepage/projects/MISMART/EightIntell.htm.

[6] Interview with Neil MacQueen, March 24, 1999

[7] Neil MacQueen and Melissa Armstrong-Hansche, *The Workshop Rotation Model: The Manual,* Revised Edition, July 1998, www.rotation.org.

[8] MacQueen, p. 19.

[9] Interview with Leslee Alfano, April 8 &15,1999

Chapter 7

[1] From an interview with Dr. John W. Grant, Aug 10, 1999.

[2] Matthew 18:3–4, Mark 9:37; 10:15, Luke 17:2, etc.

[3] William Easum, *Dancing with Dinosaurs: Ministry in a Hostile and Hurting World.* Nashville: Abingdon, 1993, p. 112.

4 *The Kairos Document: Challenge to the Church* (A Theological Comment on the Political Crisis in South Africa) Second edition, Braamfontein, South Africa, Skotaville Publishers, 1986, p. 29.

[5] *Kairos,* p. 15.

[6] Easum, *Dinosaurs,* p. 30.

[7] Henri Nouwen, *¡Gracias! A Latin American Journal,* San Francisco: Harper and Row, 1983, p. 173.

[8] Nouwen, p. 173.

Chapter 8

[1] *Taking the Temperature,* A Report from the Executive of B.C. Conference, The United Church of Canada, 1999.

[2] Robert Wuthnow, *The Crisis in the Churches: Spiritual Malaise, Financial Woe,* New York: Oxford University Press, 1997, p. 84.

[3] Loren Mead, *The Once and Future Church,* Bethesda, MD: The Alban Institute, 1991, p. 53

[4] William Chris Hobgood, *The Once and Future Pastor: The Changing Role of Religious Leaders,* Bethesda, MD: The Alban Institute, 1998, p. 24.

[5] Thomas C. Reeves, *The Empty Church: Does Organized Religion Matter Anymore?* New York: Simon & Schuster, 1998, pp.198–200

[6] Interview with Herbert O'Driscoll, December 1998.

[7] Interview with Bishop Terry Finlay, January 1999.

[8] Michael Fullan, "Emotion and Hope: Constructive Concepts for Complex Times," from *Rethinking Educational Change with Heart and Mind*, yearbook of the Association for Supervision and Curriculum Development, Alexandria, VA: ASCD, 1997.

[9] 1 Corinthians 13:4–7.

Chapter 9

[1] "Troubled Times at Beaver House," *The United Church Observer*, April 1994, p. 36.

[2] Ursula Franklin, from a speech delivered at a Ten Days for Global Justice seminar, Toronto, Canada, 1998.

[3] Franklin, speech.

[4] Telephone call from Linda Stemp, April 1999.

[5] Roy Oswald and Robert E. Friedrich, Jr., *Discerning Your Congregation's Future: A Strategic and Spiritual Approach,* Bethesda, MD: The Alban Institute, 1996, p. 166.

[6] Daniel 6:26 b

[7] Exodus 14.

[8] Oswald and Friedrich, p. x.

[9] Oswald and Friedrich, p. xii.

[10] Martin Marty, *A Short History of Christianity,* Minneapolis: Fortress, 1987, p. 185.

Chapter 10

[1] William Greider, *One World Ready or Not: The Manic Logic of Global Capitalism*, New York: Touchstone, 1998, p. 70.

[2] Richard Gwyn, "Home and Away," *The Toronto Star*, April 28 1999, p. A17

[3] Greider, p. 65.

[4] Jeremy Rifkin, *The End of Work: The Decline of the Global Labor Force and the Dawn of the Post-Market Era,* New York: Tarcher/Putnam, Putnam Group, 1995, p. 5.

[5] William Wolman and Anne Colamosca, *The Judas Economy: The Triumph of Capital and the Betrayal of Work,* New York: Addison-Wesley, 1997, p. 52.

[6] George Soros, *The Crisis of Global Capitalism, Open Society Endangered,* New York: Public

Affairs, 1998 pp. xx, xxii, xxvii.

[7] Wolman and Colamosca, pp. 88, 99.

[8] Jim Stanford, *Paper Boom: Why Real Prosperity Requires A New Approach to Canada's Economy*, The Canadian Centre for Policy Alternatives, Toronto & Ottawa: James Lorimer, 1999, p. 23.

[9] Stanford, p. 311.

[10] Loren B. Mead, *Financial Meltdown in the Mainline*, Bethesda, MD: The Alban Institute, 1998, p. 50.

[11] Francis Fukuyama, "The Great Disruption," *The Atlantic Monthly*, May 1999, p. 30.

[12] Robert Wuthnow, *The Crisis in the Churches: Spiritual Malaise, Financial Woe*, New York: Oxford University Press, 1997, p. 231.

[13] Wuthnow, p. 239.

[14] Gordon Powers, "Ethical Investing Has a Long Way To Go," *Globe and Mail*, July 10, 1999, p. B8.

[15] Stanford, p. 383.

[16] Soros, p. 197.

[17] David Morris, "Small is Still Beautiful," from *The Utne Reader*, May/June 1999, p. 24.

[18] Murray MacAdam, editor, *From Corporate Greed to Common Good: Canadian Churches and Community Economic Development*, Ottawa: Novalis, 1998 p. 18-19.

Chapter 11

[1] Walter Brueggemann, *Biblical Perspectives on Evangelism: Living in a Three-Storied Universe*, Nashville: Abingdon, 1993, p. 11.

[2] Loren B. Mead, *The Once and Future Church: Reinventing the Congregation for a New Mission Frontier*, Bethesda, MD: The Alban Institute, 1991, p. 58.

[3] All quotations from an interview with Katharine Hockin, 1991. Some of this material was first quoted in Donna Sinclair, *Crossing Worlds: The Story of the Woman's Missionary Society of the United Church of Canada*, Toronto: United Church Publishing House, 1992.

[4] Letter from Victoria Cheung to WMS, July 9, 1940, United Church Archives.

[5] Letter from T.A. Broadfoot to Edith Mckenzie, Dec.17, 1947, United Church Archives.

[6] Correspondence, Victoria Cheung, South China, United Church Archives.

[7] Letter from Dawn Vaneyk to Donna Sinclair, February 2, 1999.

[8] Vaneyk, December 17, 1998.

[9] Luke 6:20–22.

Chapter 12

[1] Donald Harman Akenson, *Surpassing Wonder: The Invention of the Bible and the Talmuds,* McGill-Queens University Press, Montreal & Kingston, 1998, p. 540.

[2] Akenson, pp. 540–542.

[3] Interview with Karen Hamilton, May 20 1999.

[4] Marcus Borg & N.T. Wright, *The Meaning of Jesus: Two Visions,* San Francisco: HarperSan Francisco, 1998. p. x.

[5] William Easum, *Dancing with Dinosaurs,* Nashville: Abingdon, 1993, *p. 88.*

[6] Easum, p. 88.

[7] Marva Dawn, *Reaching Out Without Dumbing Down,* Grand Rapids: Eerdmans 1995, p. 76.

[8] Dawn, pp. 88–89.

[9] William Easum and Thomas G Bandy, *Growing Spiritual Redwoods,* Nashville: Abingdon Press, 1997, p. 71.

[10] "Quotes and Comments," *The United Church Observer,* June 1999, p. 50.

[11] Dawn, p. 107.

[12] *Edges,* www.nexxus.bc.ca/Edges, June 16, 1999.

Closing Thoughts

[1] 1 Samuel 5:12

Bibliography

Akenson, Donald Harman. *Surpassing Wonder: The Invention of the Bible and the Talmuds.* Montreal & Kingston: McGill-Queen's University Press, 1998.

Armstrong, Donald, editor. *The Truth about Jesus.* Grand Rapids: Eerdmans, 1998.

Barna, George. *The Frog in the Kettle.* Ventura, CA: GL Publications, 1990.

Bass, Dorothy C. *Practicing our Faith: A Way of Life for a Searching People.* San Francisco: Jossey-Bass, 1997.

Bibby, Reginald. *There's Got to be More! Connecting Churches & Canadians.* Winfield, BC: Wood Lake Books, 1995.
—— *Unknown Gods: The Ongoing Story of Religion in Canada,* Toronto: Stoddart, 1993.
—— *Mosaic Madness: The Poverty and Potential of Life in Canada.* Toronto: Stoddart, 1990.

Borg, Marcus, J. *Meeting Jesus Again for the First Time: The Historical Jesus & the Heart of Contemporary Faith.* San Francisco: HarperSanFrancisco, 1994.
—— & N.T. Wright. *The Meaning of Jesus: Two Visions.* San Francisco: HarperSanFrancisco, 1998.

Brueggemann, Walter. *Biblical Perspectives on Evangelism: Living in a Three-Storied Universe.* Nashville: Abingdon, 1993.

Burnham, Sophy. *The Ecstatic Journey: The Transforming Power of Mystical Experience.* New York: Ballantine Books, 1997.

Carothers, J. Edward. *The Paralysis of Mainstream Protestant Leadership.* Nashville: Abingdon, 1990.

Crossan, John Dominic. *The Historical Jesus: The Life of a Mediterranean Jewish Peasant.* San Francisco: HarperSanFrancisco, 1991.

Dawn, Marva J. *Is It a Lost Cause? Having the Heart of God for the Church's Children.* Grand Rapids: Eerdmans, 1997.
—— *Reaching Out Without Dumbing Down: A Theology of Worship for the Turn of the Century Culture.* Grand Rapids: Eerdmans, 1995.

de Waal, Esther. *Every Earthly Blessing: Celebrating a Spirituality of Creation.* Ann Arbor, MI: Charis, 1992.

Easum, William. *Sacred Cows Make Gourmet Burgers: Ministry Anytime, Anywhere, by Anyone.* Nashville: Abingdon, 1995.
—— *Dancing with Dinosaurs: Ministry in a Hostile and Hurting World.* Nashville: Abingdon, 1993.
—— & Thomas Bandy. *Growing Spiritual Redwoods.* Nashville: Abingdon, 1997.

Fogarty, Robin & James Bellanca. *Multiple Intelligences: A Collection.* Palatine, IL: IRI/ Skylight, 1995.

Foot, David K. *Boom, Bust & Echo: How to Profit from the Coming Demographic Shift.* Toronto: Stoddart, 1997.

Friesen, John W. *You Can't Get There From Here: The Mystique of North American Plains Indians' Culture and Philosophy,* Dubuque, IO: Kendall/Hunt, 1995.

Galbraith, John Kenneth. *The Culture of Contentment.* New York: Houghton Mifflin, 1992.

Gallagher, Winifred. *Working on God.* New York: Random House, 1999.

George, Carl F. *How to Break Growth Barriers: Capturing Overlooked Opportunities for Church Growth.* Grand Rapids: Baker Book House, 1993.
—— *Prepare Your Church for the Future.* Grand Rapids: Revell, division of Baker Book House, 1991.

Graham, Rochelle, and Wayne Irwin, Flora Litt. *Healing from the Heart: A Guide to Christian Healing for Individuals and Groups.* Kelowna, BC: Wood Lake Books, 1998.

Grieder, William. *One World, Ready or Not: The Manic Logic of Global Capitalism.* New York: Touchstone, 1998.

Hadaway, C. Kirk & David A. Roozen. *Rerouting the Protestant Mainstream: Source of Growth and Opportunities for Change.* Nashville: Abingdon, 1995.

Hall, Douglas John. *Remembered Voices: Reclaiming the Legacy of "Neo-Orthodoxy."* Louisville: Westminster John Knox Press, 1998.

Harpur, Tom. *The Uncommon Touch: An Investigation of Spiritual Healing.* Toronto: McClelland & Stewart, 1994.

Hauerwas, Stanley & William Willimon. *Resident Aliens: Life in the Christian Colony.* Nashville: Abingdon, 1989.

Hobgood, William. *The Once and Future Pastor: The Changing Role of Religious Leaders.* Bethesda, MD: Alban Institute, 1998.

Hunter, George G. III. *Church for the Unchurched.* Nashville: Abingdon, 1996.

Johnson, Luke Timothy. *The Real Jesus.* San Francisco: HarperSanFrancisco, 1996.

The Kairos Document: Challenge to the Church (A Theological Comment on the Political Crisis in South Africa) Second edition. Braamfontein, South Africa: Skotaville Publishers, 1986.

Kennedy, Paul. *Preparing for the Twenty-First Century.* HarperCollins, 1993.

Lamott, Anne. *Traveling Mercies: Some Thoughts on Faith.* New York: Pantheon Books, division of Random House, 1999.

Levan, Christopher. *God Hates Religion: How the Gospels Condemn False Religious Practice.* Toronto: United Church Publishing House, 1995.

MacAdam, Murray, editor. *From Corporate Greed to Common Good: Canadian Churches and Community Economic Development.* Ottawa: Novalis, 1998.

McLeod, Bruce. *City Sermons: Preaching from a Downtown Church.* Burlington, ON: Welch Publishing, 1986.

McQuaig, Linda. *The Cult of Impotence: Selling the Myth of Powerlessness in the Global Economy.* Toronto: Viking Penguin, 1998.

MacQueen, Neil. *Computers, Kids and Christian Education*. Minneapolis: Augsburg Fortress, 1998.

—— and Melissa Armstrong-Hansche. *The Workshop Rotation Model: The Manual,* Revised Edition, July 1998, www.rotation.org.

Marty, Martin. *A Short History of Christianity,* Minneapolis: Fortress, 1987.

Mead, Loren B. *Financial Meltdown in the Mainline,* Bethesda, MD: Alban Institute, 1998.

—— *Five Challenges for the Once and Future Church.* Bethesda, MD: Alban Institute, 1996.

—— *Transforming Congregations for the Future.* Bethesda, MD: Alban Institute, 1994.

—— *The Once and Future Church: Reinventing the Congregation for a New Mission Frontier.* Bethesda, MD: Alban Institute, 1991.

Meier, John P. *A Marginal Jew: Rethinking the Historical Jesus: the Roots of the Problem and the Person.* New York: Doubleday, 1991.

"Mending the World: An Ecumenical Vision for Healing and Reconcilation," *Record of Proceedings,* 36th General Council. Toronto: The United Church of Canada, 1997.

Miller, J. R. *Shingwauk's Vision.* Toronto: University of Toronto Press, 1996.

Moore, Peter C., editor. *Can a Bishop be Wrong?* Harrisburg, PA: Morehouse, 1998.

Nouwen, Henri J.M. *¡Gracias! A Latin American Journal.* New York: Harper & Row, 1983.

Oswald, Roy and Robert E. Friedrich, Jr. *Discerning Your Congregation's Future: A Strategic and Spiritual Approach.* Bethesda, MD: The Alban Institute, 1996.

Peterson, Eugene H. *Under The Unpredictable Plant: An Exploration in Vocational Holiness.* Grand Rapids: Eerdmans, 1992.

Posterski, Don & Gary Nelson. *Future Faith Churches: Reconnecting with the Power of the Gospel for the 21st Century.* Winfield, BC: Wood Lake Books, 1997.

Posterski, Don & Irwin Barker. *Where's a Good Church?* Winfield, BC: Wood Lake Books, 1993.

Reeves, Thomas C. *The Empty Church: Does Organized Religion Matter Anymore?* New York: Simon & Schuster, 1998.

Reid, Angus. *Shakedown: How the New Economy is Shaping our Lives.* Toronto: Doubleday Canada, 1996.

Rifkin, Jeremy. *The End of Work: The Decline of the Global Labor Force and the Dawn of the Post-Market Era.* New York: Tarcher/Putnam, Putnam Group, 1995.

Ruether, Rosemary Radford. *Gaia and God: An Ecofeminist Theology of Earth Healing.* New York: HarperCollins, 1992.

Schaller, Lyle. *It's a Different World! The Challenge for Today's Pastors.* Nashville: Abingdon, 1997
—— *Tattered Trust: Is There Hope for Your Denomination?* Nashville: Abingdon, 1996.
—— *21 Bridges to the 21st Century: The Future of Pastoral Ministry.* Nashville: Abingdon, 1994.
—— *The Seven-Day-a-Week Church.* Nashville: Abingdon, 1992.
—— *The Middle Sized Church: Problems and Prescriptions.* Nashville: Abingdon, 1985.

Sine, Tom. *Wild Hope.* Waco, TX: Word, 1991.

Soros, George. *The Crisis of Global Capitalism: Open Society Endangered.* New York: Public Affairs, Perseus Books Group, 1998.

Spong, John Shelby. *Why Christianity Must Change or Die: A Bishop Speaks to Believers in Exile.* San Francisco: HarperSanFrancisco, 1998.
—— *Liberating the Gospels: Reading the Bible with Jewish Eyes: Freeing Jesus from 2000 Years of Misunderstanding.* San Francisco: HarperSanFrancisco, 1996.

Stanford, James. *Paper Boom: Why Real Prosperity Requires A New Approach to Canada's Economy.* The Canadian Centre for Policy Alternatives, Toronto & Ottawa: James Lorimer & Company, 1999.

Wagamese, Richard. *A Quality of Light.* Toronto: Doubleday Canada, 1997.

Warren, Rick. *The Purpose Driven Church: Growth without Compromising your Message & Mission.* Grand Rapids: Zondervan, 1995.

Wilkens, Michael J., and J.P. Moreland, editors. *Jesus Under Fire: Modern Scholarship Reinvents the Historical Jesus.* Grand Rapids: Zondervan, 1995.

Willimon, William H. *What's Right with the Church*. San Francisco: Harper & Row, 1985; republished New Orleans: Insight, 1998.

Wolman, William & Anne Colamosca. *The Judas Economy: The Triumph of Capital and the Betrayal of Work*. New York: Addison-Wesley, 1997.

Wright, Timothy. *A Community of Joy: How to Create Contemporary Worship*. Nashville: Abingdon, 1994.

Wuthnow, Robert. *The Crisis in the Churches: Spiritual Malaise, Financial Woe?* New York: Oxford University Press, 1997.